I Want a Baby,
He Doesn't

I Want a Baby, He Doesn't

How Both Partners Can Make
the Right Decision at the Right Time

Donna J. Wade
with Liberty Kovacs, Ph.D., M.F.T.

Adams Media
Avon, Massachusetts

Published by
Adams Media, an F+W Publications Company
57 Littlefield Street, Avon, MA 02322. U.S.A.
www.adamsmedia.com

ISBN: 1-59337-287-6

Printed in Canada.

J I H G F E D C B A

Library of Congress Cataloging-in-Publication Data
Wade, Donna J.
I want a baby, he doesn't / Donna J. Wade with Liberty Kovacs.
p.   cm.
ISBN 1-59337-287-6
1. Parenthood—Decision making. 2. Pregnancy—Decision making.
3. Family size—Decision making. 4. Married people—Psychology.
5. Marriage. I. Kovacs, Liberty. II. Title.
HQ755.8.W32 2005
646.7'8—dc22
2004025948

This publication is designed to provide accurate and authoritative information with regard to the subject matter covered. It is sold with the understanding that the publisher is not engaged in rendering legal, accounting, or other professional advice. If legal advice or other expert assistance is required, the services of a competent professional person should be sought.

—From a *Declaration of Principles* jointly adopted by a Committee of the American Bar Association and a Committee of Publishers and Associations

Many of the designations used by manufacturers and sellers to distinguish their products are claimed as trademarks. Where those designations appear in this book and Adams Media was aware of a trademark claim, the designations have been printed with initial capital letters.

This book is available at quantity discounts for bulk purchases.
For information, please call 1-800-872-5627.

This book is dedicated to my wonderful husband, Ken, for his eternal love, patience, and understanding, and for his encouragement to share our experiences in this book.

–Donna J. Wade

As a marriage and family therapist for thirty-seven years, I wish to dedicate my involvement in this book to all the courageous couples who have experienced and who are experiencing the challenges and struggles portrayed here. I am deeply touched and moved by the bravery and persistence of couples caught up in the dilemma of whether to have children. I admire your dauntless determination to work together and to achieve the ultimate intimate relationship.

–Liberty Kovacs, Ph.D., M.F.T.

Acknowledgments

Several people contributed their encouragement as I was writing this book. Through their support I was given the initial strength and courage to write about my husband's and my intensely personal decision to have children, which was revealed in my first version of *I Want a Baby, He Doesn't*.

Many thanks go to our minister, Carol Lunde, and our good friends Ed and Carol Brown for volunteering their time and feedback on the first draft of my book proposal. They were the foundation of energy that gave this book life.

Special thanks go to Dolores Mandziara, Karen Sheldon, Debbie Picard, Lisa Hebert, Sylvia McCleary, Paulette Peerenboom, Sarah Kidder, Patricia Hurzeler, Xavier and Caroline De Weck, Susie Makin, Dr. Alfred and Anita Vaucher, Dr. Dominic De Ziegler and his nurse Esther Schärer, and the late Rena Zoren for their emotional support throughout my fertility treatments and their incredible devotion in volunteering to read and give invaluable advice and pointers throughout the development of my first version of this book.

I still thank God for Paulette Peerenboom, one of the best neighbors I've ever had, whom I appreciate dearly for giving me a Pergonal shot when Ken was out of town on business.

A special thanks to my mom. Thank you for listening to me when I needed you most. There are times when only a mother's understanding and support can give comfort to a daughter.

I am grateful to my first editor, Mary Inderstrodt, Kendra Joseph, and Trafford Publishing for helping me produce a book that Adams Media was excited about. A very special thanks goes to Jeffrey Rubin Morey, Ph.D., Dr. Thomas Elardo, Dr. Stacey Hein, Dr. Amy Allen, Monika Sujczynska, Christopher Hickey, L.M.F.T., and Therese Sorrentino, MFT, for helping me promote the first version of my book, *I Want a Baby, He Doesn't*.

Many warm thanks go to all the people we interviewed, who generously bared their souls to share their experiences in an effort to help others. Each of you knows who you are and I am sincerely thankful and grateful to you for sharing your stories so that others can learn. You are clearly role models.

Thank you to RESOLVE for their support on infertility and for their outstanding educational seminars on adoption that we have mentioned in this book. A special thanks goes to Kris Allen, a RESOLVE Support Leader, for connecting me with a number of adoptive parents who have shared the adoption experiences that are in this book.

Many thanks to Planned Parenthood for allowing us to use their "How to Be a Good Parent" questionnaire, located in the appendix of this book. Thank you to Roland C. Warren, president of the National Fatherhood Initiative, for the use of statistical fatherhood facts by Wade F. Horn, Ph.D., and Tom Sylvester. I would also like to thank Random House for granting us permission to use statistical information on marital satisfaction after children from their book, *The Transition to Parenthood: How a First Child . . .* by Jay Belsky, Ph.D., and John Kelly.

A heartfelt thanks goes to everyone in Ken's family, every person in mine, and to all our friends, for their incredible support throughout the rewrite to produce this book, and for their enduring understanding when I could not be in attendance at gatherings.

Thank you to Adams Media for calling me on my birthday and giving me one of the best birthday surprises I've ever had, by inviting me to rewrite my book, *I Want a Baby, He Doesn't*, and for teaming me up with one of the most outstanding women I know, Liberty Kovacs, Ph.D., M.F.T. Dr. Kovacs, thank you for your gift of advice, counsel, edit, and most of all, your friendship. I am grateful for the opportunity to have worked with you and to be your friend.

A very special thanks to Kate Epstein and Bridget Brace, at Adams Media, for their editorial genius, their unwavering belief in me, their incredible drive to help me produce an outstanding version of *I Want a Baby, He Doesn't*, and for helping me realize my dream of getting this book into the hands of the public. Thank you, Kate and Bridget, I am eternally grateful.

And most of all, I'd like to thank my incredible husband, Ken, for whom I'm eternally grateful. Many nights he went to bed alone while I remained at my computer writing. Without his infinite love, support, and motivation, this book would not have been possible. Thank you, sweetheart. I love you.

All of the examples in this book are true and accurate. However, to protect the privacy of people mentioned in this book, their names have been changed. The only peoples' names that remain identifiable are my husband's and my own.

Contents

Introduction

I fell in love with and married my husband, Ken, within one year of meeting him. He is the man of my dreams. Throughout our whirlwind courtship, we touched upon the subject of children, but we never really resolved our differences while dating. I desperately wanted children with Ken, but he had gotten a vasectomy before we met. I recall that on the eve of our engagement Ken said he would get a reverse vasectomy. After our wedding, he said he had no recollection of ever uttering those words.

During our first year of marriage, we experienced multiple ups and downs on the "baby issue"—which is the subject of this book. The realization of being childless and not even having the option to have children was a startling one for me. I have never before experienced such deep sorrow and feelings of loss. The internal pain, one that only a woman can know, threw me into a dark depression that lasted six long months. Finding another man was not an option. I wouldn't have wanted it; there was, and still is, simply too much love between Ken and me to give up. This issue prompted the beginning of our many long discussions on children.

With virtually no resources to assist me other than my communication and facilitation skills, I persevered in trying to convince Ken that children would enrich our marriage. I talked with a trusted friend, and she said "Good luck!" adding that she felt my husband was now scum for not wanting to make my dreams come true. That wasn't what I wanted to hear. I knew then that I couldn't even talk to my own family for fear they would resent Ken. I combed the library and bookstores for help—nothing! After months of frustration, I realized that the two things we had going for us were my facilitation skills and our respect for each other. We used these assets as building blocks in our attempt to reach a mutual resolution.

Not knowing the odds were against me for Ken to get a reverse vasectomy, I continued to discuss the option with him. We had two major roadblocks, though. First, he needed to come to terms with his own feelings on children and to recognize my need for a child. Second, I wanted Ken to honestly want to get a reversal. I emphasized that he needed to feel that his desire to have a child was stronger than his desire to please me. I knew intuitively that if he made the decision to have a baby just to appease me, our marriage could very likely be in jeopardy after children entered the picture.

While my husband and I struggled with our opposing views, we talked . . . and talked . . . and talked. We even baby-sat my nieces and nephews, visited professionals, and listened to other couples who were experiencing similar difficulty. I thought it would be beneficial to know why some couples were more successful than others in reaching a mutually satisfying agreement.

Throughout our ordeal, we stayed focused through our opposing views on children and shared our problem as a team. We discussed our childhoods, we listened to each other's views and interests, and we shared why it was so important for each of us to have children or to remain child-free. I frequently took notes to help me remain calm and objective, and Ken and I agreed to take breaks when things got a little heated. When we were at a stalemate, we sought help through a counselor. Unfortunately, the counselor we chose was a crisis counselor and wasn't trained to deal with our type of problem, so we opted to keep trying to resolve our issue on our own.

What Ken and I went through and learned needs to be shared with others so that anyone in a similar situation never has to feel alone or without options. The result of our many discussions and personal outcomes, along with discussions with other couples, was presented in my original version of *I Want a Baby, He Doesn't*.

Three years later, Adams Media teamed me up with Liberty Kovacs, Ph.D., M.F.T., and helped me convert my original version into the book you are currently reading.

Our focus is on how you and your partner can overcome your differences about when and if to start a family. The decision to have children, and when to have them, is probably one of the most life-altering decisions you will make. For some couples, this decision comes naturally and easily, but for many other couples, the decision whether to have children can be an emotional battle, sometimes costing them their relationships.

Dr. Kovacs and I have included a variety of different situations that people may encounter in various stages of their relationships—from how and when to begin to talk about children, to having another child in a second marriage. We interviewed a number of people who generously agreed to share their experiences so that you can learn from their examples. These people shared some of the most intimate and emotionally challenging times of their lives and we thank them for their generosity and trust. From these interviews, we learned that the baby issue was complicated by age and fertility and so we decided to address these issues as well.

We also found many other factors, including:

+ A decidedly large number of men have fears about children and these fears translated into procrastination about having children. This has become a big issue in today's world, where it is commonplace for couples to have two-career families while they are practicing birth control of some form. Although this setup has allowed many couples to obtain the lifestyle they desire while postponing children until the "optimal" time, the problem arises when the couple disagrees about when that time is. While birth control has given women a greater degree of freedom in making choices about family, that freedom can bring emotional, and possibly medical, complexities to the decision.

+ Additional disagreements arise among couples that already have children—one partner wants to expand the family with another child and the other partner is opposed. These problems are equally as complex as the problems experienced by couples trying to have their first child.

+ Women in the last stages of their fertile years tend to realize their hopes of ever having a baby are fading away. They feel that unless they take immediate action, their dreams of becoming a parent will never be realized. This highly emotional state can have serious implications. Relationships are negatively affected when one of the partners has reluctantly accepted a child-free life, or when one partner is faced with infertility and is not willing to undergo necessary infertility treatments.

+ A number of couples in their second marriages face difficulties in blending their families and in desiring to have a child of their own. Blended families have enough complexities, let alone adding another child to the mix.

During the time Ken and I were working through our differences on children, I always told him that I would never pursue infertility treatments. But, no woman can say how she will react, until faced with the fact that she has a fertility issue (and the same issue exists for men). For those couples that have postponed children to the point where science needs to intervene, I've included the experiences Ken and I had with fertility treatments to give you a better idea of what to expect if you find yourselves in this situation.

Dr. Kovacs adds her years of experience in analyzing the couples' scenarios presented here. She has also helped apply her integrated developmental and family systems model of adult relationships to demonstrate how experiences in childhood affect decisions and responses in adult relationships. Through her observation of couples that have contributed their stories, Dr. Kovacs gives insightful advice for others.

Dr. Kovacs and I also offer a section on suggested reading, organizations, and Web sites that may be of help. Planned Parenthood has allowed us to include a questionnaire on parenting, "How to Be a Good Parent," (see page 191). Taking this test may highlight some issues you have and help you understand the responsibilities of becoming a parent.

For many couples, having children can be an easy decision. But my husband and I faced indecision, vasectomy reversal, decision, fertility testing, infertility treatments, and adoption. Through it all, and most important, we grew as a couple. Ken and I decided to try to have children; your decision will be complex, and it may take you in a different direction than ours did, but I hope that you, too, will experience growth in your relationship. Ken and I have been married more than ten years and attribute our happiness and success to how we dealt with our disagreement on whether to have children. Whenever we have an issue that we don't see eye-to-eye on, we utilize skills learned from overcoming our differences on children. With this book, *I Want a Baby, He Doesn't*, Dr. Kovacs and I hope to give you the fundamentals that can help you successfully get through what can be an emotionally challenging phase of your life.

Part I

Approaching the Subject

Chapter 1

How to Begin
Talking about Children

Love is filled with decisions, choices, and changes. In the courtship phase, we decide whether to go on a second, third, or fourth date. Later on, we decide whether to continue the relationship and explore the depth of interest and possibilities it may bring. As the relationship progresses, we continue to ask ourselves questions to ensure we are making the right choice. Is this person the right match for me? Are our interests in alignment? Is this the person I want to marry, that I want to have children with?

As women, we ask ourselves questions like this while we're falling in love. After all, most of us have been planning our weddings since the age of five. But when is the right time to begin talking about children with the man of your dreams?

If the subject of children is not discussed at some point, then you are leaving the relationship open to dangerous assumptions by both parties. Liberty Kovacs, Ph.D., with more than thirty years as a marital therapist, has developed guidelines for looking at problems and a system to track the relationship as it evolves. Her guidelines and theories on family systems and adult development are found throughout this book. Simply put, often the issues that occur within a relationship can be traced back to some unresolved past event. Left unresolved, these issues can continue to prevent a partner from moving forward in a relationship and block that person from reaching a solution—which, in this book, includes the decision on children.

If you met through computer dating or a matchmaking service, you may know up-front if your partner is open to children. But "open" can have its ambiguities. And quite often, you may not know at all what he wants. You already know that you want children, but what about him? How does he feel? How and when do you ask him about his feelings toward children? Do you just come right out and ask, how do you feel about having children some day? Pose this question too early in the relationship, and you may find your date running off so fast that you'll be left in a smoke trail. If you wait too long to ask your partner how he feels about children, and he reveals that he doesn't want any, you may run the risk of being too emotionally involved at that point to make a rational decision about the future of your relationship.

Perhaps you have a screening technique, like Brenda did with her dates. She started out by asking her date about his childhood, his family, and then his feelings on children. If her date came from a close-knit family, had fond memories as a child, and envisioned a family of his own, then she considered him second-date material. This was Brenda's way of protecting herself from getting involved with the "wrong" man and ensuring that she would realize her goal of having a family.

It's crucial to communicate your desires early in the relationship. For one, you can make an informed decision about the future of your relationship without investing a large amount of time and emotion. The early stage, while you are exploring each other's interests, is probably the best time to discover if you are on the same page regarding children.

Before you start asking him questions about his feelings, make sure you know *your* mind. How do you know if you're ready to have children? Ask yourself, "What's important about having children to me?" Knowing what's important about having children will give you a greater understanding of the degree of your own desire. Fully understanding your own mindset will allow you to express yourself in a clear manner, which is important when discussing matters of this magnitude.

This is an area where you never want to misrepresent yourself. For example, if you know in your heart that you strongly want children, do not say "Maybe" if he asks you. This answer gives the indication that you do not have a burning desire to have children and that you consider the topic of children casual. It can also give the impression that living child-free would be acceptable to you. Make it clear that you are not merely "open" to having children, but you actively desire them. If you know that children are an absolute must in your life, be honest and up-front.

To get him talking, a casual question about his childhood will help you discern if he has happy memories. Later, deeper questions can be worked into the conversation while talking about personal dreams and goals. While he's talking, ask him, "Do you think that you'll ever have a family?" Or, "Do you see yourself ever having a family?" You're not asking him to marry you or to have children with you—you're simply finding out if he's interested in having children some day.

These questions allow for a simple yes or no answer. If you would like him to elaborate on his response, you can ask, "What's important about having a family to you?" Or if he answered no to your first question, you can ask, "What's important about not having a family to you?" These open-ended questions will get him talking about his feelings about children. By knowing the answers to these questions, you can move forward with confidence in your relationship or decide he's not the one for you and dump him.

New Relationships

According to Virginia Satir, an early founder of family therapy, your relationship begins the first time you set eyes on each other.[1] You're fascinated with each other, and your mutual hobbies, exotic travels, and respective jobs and ambitions. Everything is new and exciting. Most of all, you actively listen to each other's interests, hopes, and problems. You feel magnetized to each other. You feel that you've found a true friend who cares, someone you can trust. As a result, in most cases, love blossoms and you experience a euphoric lovesick state.

Yes, falling in love actually stimulates the brain's production of a chemical called phenylethylamine, which provides a euphoric feeling.[2] Even if you're still technically single, this is considered the romance stage and the first stage of marriage. For up to two years, new love can turn people into lovesick fools who believe that everything is wonderful, that their partner is flawless, that they will live together in happiness forever, and that nothing could ever destroy their strong feelings of affection. During this euphoric phase, couples may make promises that they cannot recall later on.

My husband and I were one such couple. Ken was divorced, had had no children with his first wife, and had gotten a vasectomy before we met. I had never been married and wanted children. We fell in love, and within a few months Ken proposed. I knew he was the one, so I said yes. Later that night, over dinner, I asked Ken, "What about children? You know how I feel about wanting to have a family." Ken responded, "I'll just get a reverse vasectomy." I was so happy! The man of my dreams had just asked me to marry him and also promised to get a reverse vasectomy so that we could have children. Ken was also ecstatic. The woman he had given his heart to had said yes to his proposal of marriage.

We married six months later. After the honeymoon, I approached Ken about setting a date for his reverse vasectomy. He was surprised. He didn't recall ever agreeing to have the procedure. A long period of discussions, questions, and soul-searching followed. We took almost a full year to reach an amicable agreement, but not before the blindness of new love had almost led us in completely opposite directions. Ken initially envisioned us with a child-free life while I was forecasting a family with him.

During this "lovesick" phase, some people may agree to things they normally would not. One of those agreements may be to have children. To ensure that your partner is fully aware of his newly stated promise, and to avoid a situation similar to what Ken and I went through, revisit the conversation about children the following day, or even the following week. Don't put it off too long. He needs to know your excitement level on this subject, and you need to know that he is sincere. You may want to bring up the topic of children again by asking him to be more specific: "When do you see us starting a family?" This way you can find out whether his initial response was phenylethylamine induced.

Existing Relationships

You've already established your relationship. You're committed to each other, either engaged, living together, or married. This is the second stage of your relationship or marriage, which is filled with expectations and compromises. Both of you value your commitment and love each other very much. You feel somewhat comfortable or very comfortable with each other's values and beliefs. You've talked, as a team, about your roles and expectations of each other. Each of you has communicated your initial needs and desires in life, and you're currently pursuing your joint goals. If these things haven't taken place yet, you may want to think about discussing them now because, whether you realize it or not, unconscious expectations will start to surface at this stage in a relationship.

Many marriages and long-term relationships have been formed with children in mind. But, rarely do relationships mature in a way that goes according to plan. Falling in love, getting married, having children, and living happily ever after doesn't always happen in that order. Some elements may be left off that list altogether. As you and your partner travel down the path of life, initial desires and expectations can change. People grow, mature, and change, and biological clocks without snooze buttons can cause these changes. Inevitably, as the relationship grows, situations also change.

Goals related to the timing of children may be accelerated because of surprises or they may need to be put on hold a little longer after encountering life's many obstacles and challenges.

As many couples choose to do, Deborah and Michael agreed to postpone having children for a year to allow them to enjoy their relationship as a couple and to save up for a house. After they purchased the house, Michael wanted to postpone their family until after his promotion. He received his promotion but then wanted to hold off on children until after the remodel of their house. Deborah began to get worried that they might never start a family. (For more on Deborah and Michael's story, see Chapter 5, page 53.)

Conflicts like Deborah and Michael's can be unpleasant. Honesty is difficult if one or both partners come from families that do not permit open expression of feelings, wants, and needs. But when a partner decides to table her desires for children just to avoid conflict, she risks harboring resentment. And when that resentment surfaces, the man may be baffled—he believed the issue was resolved. Openness and honesty is the best policy at all times.

With the evolution of the relationship, some people find that their original wants and desires change. All relationships experience change, and sometimes that change is about the desire to have children, as it was for Charlotte and John.

Charlotte and John met, fell in love, and married. Initially, Charlotte did not want to have children. She was a marketing manager and wanted to focus on her career and her marriage. When Charlotte turned thirty-five, she found she suddenly had an overwhelming urge to have children. Most of her friends were married and had toddlers or newborns. Her brother was married and had a baby boy. Each time she held her nephew or a friend's baby, her maternal instincts seemed to grow.

Often, women will have a strong desire to have children in their mid- to late thirties, especially if they have not yet had a child. Even women with children experience the desire to have a child at this time. When Charlotte reached her mid-thirties, she realized she truly wanted to have a baby and that she fit into this scenario.

She communicated her desire to her husband. She let him know how important having a family was to her. John was deeply involved in his career as an engineer. He was content with their child-free lifestyle. Reluctantly, Charlotte agreed to remain child-free, but her strong desire to have a baby did not go away. In fact, her craving to have a child became all-consuming. Although Charlotte and John did not see eye-to-eye, the key is that they communicated their positions to each other, and continued to communicate until they could reach an amicable agreement. Finally, almost a year after Charlotte had first announced her desire for a baby, John agreed.

First Marriages

More than fifty years of research indicates that marital satisfaction declines with each child. There is high satisfaction at the beginning of the marriage, followed with a steep decline at the birth of the first child; then marital happiness increases, but it never again reaches as high as it was in the beginning. Once the child reaches adolescence, the couple experiences another decline in their wedded satisfaction level.

Although statistics indicate that more couples are opting to have only one child, there are a number of couples who want to give their first child a brother or sister who will be a buddy and best friend, someone to play with, laugh with, cry with, and grow with. Some couples may already have two children of the same sex and feel they would be completing the family by having a third, "hoping for a girl this time." Not all couples are on the same page when the urge to have another child arises.

Depending on a number of circumstances, your partner may not want to introduce more children to the marriage, as with Karen and Sean, both thirty years old. They had been married for five years and had a beautiful three-year-old girl. Both of them worked full-time while their daughter was cared for by her grandmother. Friends and family constantly asked Karen when she would have another baby. A few of her girlfriends were pregnant with their second babies, which made Karen want to get pregnant again. But Sean wanted to focus on growing his business and didn't want any more children.

Karen tried talking with Sean several times about wanting to give their daughter a baby brother or sister. His response was always a flat no, and then he wouldn't talk about the subject anymore. Feeling desperate for another child, Karen continued trying to talk with her husband.

Karen recognized that their opposing views on having another child were causing stress and communication issues in their marriage. Even though Sean didn't want to talk about the subject of another child, Karen didn't listen to him. She demonstrated her courage and strength in continuing their talks until they reached a resolution. Sean was reluctant, but he agreed to have another baby. Karen was unclear as to whether Sean's decision was made to appease her. If so, she was concerned that Sean would not accept their new baby when the child was born.

This also happened with Brenda and Tom, both in their late thirties. The pair already had a happy family with two beautiful daughters—ages six and four. Since her thirty-third birthday, Brenda had had an irresistible urge to have another baby. She desperately wanted a baby boy and she felt this would complete their family. But Tom didn't want any more children. Tom was content with their situation and didn't want to add stress to their happy life. Brenda felt she would always regret a decision not to have a third baby.

When a couple has a happy marriage filled with one or more children who enrich their relationship, it is understandable when one partner doesn't want to introduce more children to the family. Tom was fearful that adding another child would add stress and upset their current lifestyle. Taking care of three children is more expensive, a lot more work than taking care of two, and also takes a lot more emotional energy.

Brenda was aware of the additional costs and work that adding another child to their family would bring. She continued to talk with her husband about the importance of completing their family with a third child (maybe a boy this time) until they reached an agreement. Through her perseverance and open communication, Brenda was able to satisfy her desire to complete their family with another baby. After two years of discussion and a compromise, Tom finally agreed to have a third child with his wife. Their family is now complete—with three girls. Brenda and Tom welcomed their new baby girl warmly and lovingly, feeling complete with a family of three girls. (For more on Brenda and Tom's story, see Chapter 6, page 71.)

Second Marriages

A number of second marriages include children from a previous marriage, which can make the second marriage more complicated. Sometimes these marriages are to successful men who have already raised children with their first wife. They insist that their new, much younger "trophy wife" not have children, often writing this arrangement into the prenuptial agreement. In many cases, women will make the tradeoff, even though they crave children, because they are so in love with their husband and the current lifestyle they have together.

Dianne found herself in this situation with fifty-year-old Allan, a successful marketing director. Allan had two grown children from his first marriage and was insistent that Dianne, at thirty-eight, not have children. Dianne was hesitant, but agreed to this arrangement when they married, thinking, "What's more important, a great marriage or a child?" Dianne entered into the marriage with full knowledge that Allan did not want children. Caught up in a new marriage and an extravagant lifestyle, she initially convinced herself she had no desire for children.

Just a year later, her decision turned painful. She suddenly became aware of pregnant women or women pushing strollers everywhere she went. She felt pulled toward every baby. This went on for two years, a constant reminder of her own biological clock on full-tilt with no hope of becoming a mother. Dianne thought she could change her husband's mind. "If he loved me, he would allow me the opportunity to have a baby." But Dianne couldn't change Allan's mind, and she could not let go of her desire to have a baby.

Allan stood his ground and was firm with their arrangement not to have children. For him, there was no discussion. Sadly, Allan's strong opposition on children cost him their marriage. Dianne and her husband are now separated, and she recently became pregnant by artificial insemination through a sperm donor. Dianne chose single motherhood over her marriage. This is an example of how love changes as the reality of unexpressed or unknown desires begin to surface. (For more on Dianne and Allan's story, see Chapter 9, page 106.)

Sarah and Jack were also each on their second marriage. Sarah had full custody of three boys from a previous marriage, and Jack had full custody of his two girls from his first marriage. When they married, their house was full with children ranging in age from three to eight. Two years passed with some family issues, but mostly with patience, love, and understanding of a blended family; everyone adjusted well to their new lives. Then Sarah decided she wanted another baby. She felt that having another baby of their own would make their marriage whole.

Jack was stunned by Sarah's request. He had already increased his family by four just with his marriage to Sarah. Although he enjoyed his new family, he was concerned with the expense and added pressure of another child. This was the beginning of many long discussions on whether they would extend their family.

Raising a blended family can bring some painful and difficult stepfamily issues. Research on blended families indicates that the adjustment phase can take a long time and sometimes the two families never blend, particularly with preadolescent and adolescent children. Sarah and Jack overcame some of those issues during their first two years of marriage. They accepted each other's children, so there was no case of "your kids, my kids." Her wish to have a child with her husband is not uncommon in these types of situations. But bringing another child into the equation may change the dynamics of the family. For this reason, it is important that the decision is extended to the entire blended family for consensus. (For more on Sarah and Jack's story, see Chapter 7, page 88.)

As mentioned earlier, Dr. Kovacs created an Integrated Developmental and Family Systems Model that more effectively assesses problem areas and assists individuals and couples in overcoming developmental blocks, or "unfinished business." These issues start in childhood and are then played out in marital relationships. The building blocks that the Relationship or Marital Process is based on are as follows:

1. The infant's relationship with his/her parents during the first three to five years
2. The model of the parent's marriage
3. Each partner's family dynamics

Any developmental blocks can prohibit agreement on the decision to have children and may affect other areas in your life. Once the developmental blocks of the past are resolved, the couple may proceed in resolving differences and continuing with growth and development, including redesigning their relationship to fit the growth needs of both partners.

A person's childhood experiences significantly influence and shape his or her marital relationship. As a result, many people repeat their family patterns. They deal with issues the same way their parents did. This behavior feels right and familiar. But parents should not be blamed for their adult children's problems.

Each partner in a relationship comes from a different family with a different set of dynamics, and each has the tendency to want to structure the relationship to be like the one his or her parents had. This is only natural, but it can lead to frustration and conflict especially in the area of wanting or not wanting to have children.

In order to move forward, the couple needs to learn to design and rebuild their relationship to fit their own needs. To do this, they will also have to learn to communicate more effectively, identify their differences, problem solve, resolve conflicts, negotiate, and formulate solutions.

Things to remember for when and how to talk to your partner about children include the following:

+ Early in the relationship, during the romance stage, is the best time to find out whether your partner is interested in having children.
+ Raise the issue initially by asking about his life growing up; then as you become closer, ask about what he wants in a relationship.
+ If you wait too long to discuss the topic, you risk becoming too emotionally involved to make a rational decision about the future of your relationship.
+ Falling in love actually alters the brain's chemical reaction, causing you to become euphorically lovesick and to make promises that you may regret later. Try to keep your head on straight while determining if this is the man for you.

When you're in stage two of a relationship, where goals are discussed, unconscious life expectations may surface if you haven't already discussed them with your partner. For example, the timing of when you want to start a family may not be in accord with your husband's preferences. More communication is necessary to understand each other. This is also a point in a relationship where compromises are made.

When you experience opposing views on children, the conflict can be unpleasant, as was Deborah and Michael's case. Sometimes people change their minds later in life about the initial desire to have children, which can cause conflict between partners. Power struggles and control issues, which can intensify matters, usually arise later in the relationship.

In any situation, one thing is always clear: Effective communication is key to the success of relationships in which the partners are experiencing difficulty resolving differences in the decision to have children.

Chapter 2

Practical Considerations about Children

Have you ever known a couple who ventured into parenthood without thinking how a baby would impact their careers, expenses, lifestyle in retirement, or their differences in parenting roles or religious beliefs? Children can play a big role in the success or downfall of a relationship. This is why it's so important to be open and honest with your partner from the very beginning of a relationship. Communicating your emotions, along with your wants and desires in life, helps build trust—a necessary ingredient for a solid relationship. For many people, the decision to have children is often based on emotion. Not much thought is given to how this life-altering decision will affect their lives in the future.

Some women are so swept up in the emotional current with their partner that they can't think. They believe their lives should follow the fairy-tale sequence of events portrayed in many children's books: meet the man of your dreams, fall in love, marry, have children, and live happily ever after. The reality of today's society is that more women have careers, and some discover the need or desire to have a baby only after years in the marriage.

One way to communicate your emotions effectively to your partner is by sharing your values and beliefs with him, and hearing his in return, on practical considerations about children. There are a number of areas that you should examine when you are thinking of bringing children into your life, including your jobs, career growth, expenses, retirement, religion, parental roles, and the fertility or infertility of each partner. You and your partner's thoughts in each of these areas may be in alignment or in opposition.

What impact will children have on your current job or on your partner's job? Will you quit your job to stay at home and raise your children, will you rely on day care, or will you make other arrangements while you continue to work? How does your partner feel about you staying home? If you go back to work, how do you feel and how does he feel about someone else caring for your baby while the two of you are at work all day?

Ideally, it would be best for one of you to stay at home and raise your child with your values and beliefs. Unfortunately, not all families are in a financial position to support themselves with one income. If you're insistent on one of you staying home, then take a look at your budget and see what can be trimmed to make your goal a reality. You may want to compare the cost of day care with the salary that you make when you return to work. Determine if the cost difference is worth the time away from your child.

When Sandra and Ed were expecting their first child, they reviewed their current income and cash flow. Ed was earning around $48,000 a year as a construction worker, and Sandra was making about $25,000 annually as an entry-level accountant. Their expenses were roughly $2,500 a month; with their combined income, they were able to save most of Sandra's earnings. Sandra researched the licensed day-care facilities in her area. If she continued to work after their baby was born, the cost of a good-quality day care would be slightly less than her net take-home pay.

With that in mind, Sandra and Ed agreed that it would be in their best interest for Sandra to stay home and raise their new baby.

Sandra and Ed were fortunate that they were able to make the decision to raise their child with one full-time stay-at-home parent. In addition to a new baby in their lives, they will have an obvious adjustment to their income. They will need to talk about how this affects their lifestyle, savings, and how they will adapt to the changes. Instead of going out to dinner once a week, they may be able to afford outings once a month. A camping trip may take the place of a vacation in Hawaii.

Financial Costs Associated with Children

If you find yourself in a situation where having a child just may break the bank, it is critical that you talk with your partner about how you will make the upcoming adjustments. Money constraints can be a big issue in relationships, so discuss the types of changes and sacrifices each of you will make prior to the "due date." Communication makes the transition from two incomes to one easier to accept, and it helps partners adjust to new parenting roles.

There is no doubt that child care can be expensive, but plans exist to help reduce costs. Depending on where you live and the quality of day care you require, the cost per child can range from $250 to $1,250 per month. This is less than what you would pay for a nanny, but the cost of day care adds up. Employer-sponsored Flexible Spending Accounts (FSA) can help trim your child-care costs by allowing you to set aside up to $5,000 (per household per year) of your annual pretax income to pay for child care in a licensed day-care facility or care provided by a nanny. One drawback to FSAs, though, is that any money you set aside but don't use will be forfeited at the end of the calendar year.

If your employer does not offer an FSA, then you are eligible for the child-care tax credit. Your child-care tax credit is dependent on your income.[1] The lower your income is, the greater the child-care tax credit.

Participation in an FSA exempts you from the child-care tax credit. Uncle Sam allows you to participate in one or the other—but not both. To learn more about the child-care tax credit, visit the IRS Web site at *www.irs.gov.*

Other costs associated with raising a child include housing, food, transportation, health care, education, and miscellaneous items such as clothing and extracurricular costs. A 2003 Department of Agriculture report estimated that, depending on household income, parents spend between $130,000 and $261,000 for the basic needs of a child through age seventeen.[2] This figure does not even include college costs, orthodontics, or sports or music lessons.

Some costs that can add up quickly include essential baby equipment: a crib at an average of $100, a rocking chair to rock your child to sleep at $150, electrical outlet protector caps at $2 each, and other babyproofing home supplies. You'll need a stroller and car seat, which run about $200, and, depending on the size of your family, a bigger car. A semester of swim lessons can be $170, music lessons can be around $25 an hour, inline speed skates can cost up to $500 a pair, eight weeks of hockey and figure skating can cost between $75 to $250, and an aspiring ballet student's pointe shoes range from $35 to $100 a pair. These expenses continue to grow as your child ages, so be prepared and don't underestimate the costs.

Now that we've scared the bejeezus out of you with how expensive the first eighteen years of a child's life will be, here's a ray of sunshine for perspective. A person who smokes two packs of cigarettes a day, at nearly $4 a pack, over a seventeen-year period, will spend close to $50,000—a little under half of what it would cost to raise a child in that time. Raising a child is expensive and will require a change in your financial priorities, but it is usually doable with some planning and effort.

Parents who stay on budget can save significantly, especially at the newborn and toddler stage, by buying perfectly good, and sometimes new, items at secondhand stores that specialize in baby items.

Career Growth

Raising a newborn takes a lot of time and effort and can stifle your career. When you're not at the office, you're working full-time at home changing your baby's diapers, feeding her, soothing her, taking her to the doctors, playing with her, taking her to "Barney on Ice" and baby Gym-boree, getting up in the middle of the night to calm her from a crying fit—not to mention housework, cooking and cleaning, and having less and less time to go after those special projects that will get you promoted at the office.

When Julie and Tim had their first child, she decided to take a leave of absence for one year to stay home with their baby. She realized she was putting her engineering career on hold, and that once she returned it would take her a while to catch up with the latest changes in technology. Still, Julie felt the opportunity to stay home with her baby for that first year far outweighed any promotion her boss could have given her at work. How is Julie today? She's back at work as an engineer, but Julie doesn't put in the long hours at work that she once did. She would rather be at home in the evening with her family. When asked if she would have changed anything, Julie has no regrets: "Absolutely not! That was one of the most precious years of my life."

In Julie's case, her company allowed her to take a one-year sabbatical and come back to work at the same level she left. Depending on the job or specialty, some companies offer one- to five-year sabbaticals to their employees, with the promise to hire them back in a similar position with pay equal to what they received at the time they left. If you are considering a leave of absence, you may want to check with your employer to see if they offer this type of program. Regardless of your thoughts on returning to work, you should fully understand your employer's benefits program for pregnancy leave.

For many women, staying at home with their baby for the first year is only a dream. Once paid pregnancy leave (normally twelve weeks) is over, many women find themselves back at work trying to juggle a career with their new competing parenting responsibilities and family roles.

Regardless of whether you are on the career fast track, the transition back to work can be an especially stressful time for a new mother and her partner. If you choose to give your child breastmilk, there's always the possibility of having to use a breast pump at work. Many companies will assist you and make arrangements for a private location. You may find that when you reach into your briefcase to get a file, you pull out a pacifier instead. As you drive to work, you'll ask yourself, "Was it my turn to drop the baby off at day care?" "Did I remember to pack enough formula and diapers?" "Did my husband say he would pick up our baby after work?" These are just a few of the daily questions that many anxious new parents have.

Parenting Roles

Before a baby arrives, you and your partner need to agree on your new parenting roles and expectations of each other (who does what and when). Is your partner willing to get up in the middle of the night to give your baby his 2:00 A.M. feeding? Will he help change dirty diapers? Will your partner be able to miss some work if the child gets sick? What about playtime—is he willing to spend a half hour or more every day to read or play with his son?

Talk about how you were brought up as a child. What you experienced will influence how you will rear your own children. As your baby grows, will you and your partner see eye to eye on disciplining your child? Will one of you be the disciplinarian while the other is the "good" parent? Whatever you agree to in raising your child, it is important for the stability of the child that you be consistent. Communicate what you can and can't do, know your limitations, and express them so that you and your partner will know each other's expectations and how to support each other.

You may want to consider taking a parenting class if you think you are absolutely set on having children. Some pediatricians and baby specialty stores offer free parenting classes, there are online parenting classes, and some community colleges offer evening parenting classes where children may also attend. Your options for learning how to be a parent are abundant through support groups, both in your community and online. You may also want to check out your local library and favorite bookstores for parenting books—there are mountains of books on this subject! This research will give you a better understanding of what parenting will require, and you will be armed with information and questions when you discuss your options with your partner.

Retirement

Parenthood is an eye-opening experience that changes with each developmental stage in your child. If you find yourself entering into parenthood, you'll discover that transition of parenting roles will be ongoing throughout your lives, even when your child is forty-five and you're retired!

Couples in their mid-thirties and early forties who are considering having children will need to examine how having a baby at their age will affect their lifestyle in retirement. This is actually a good question for couples at any age. (Remember, children can cost as much as $261,000 through age seventeen.) If you have a baby, are you still going to be able to save for retirement? What if one of you stops working to raise your baby—will you still be able to retire in the lifestyle that you want? Unless Junior becomes a sports or entertainment superstar, it's not likely that your children will be able to help you—they will likely be going through this exercise themselves.

Many people know when they would like to retire and how much money they would like to have when they retire, but less than 20 percent of us will retire in the lifestyle that we desire. This is why planning for retirement is the number-one concern of Americans today. For more information on retirement planning, you may want to check out your local library or bookstores, or see a financial planning professional when you are discussing children with your partner.

Religion

Do you and your partner have differing views on religion? If so, can these differences be overcome without feeling that you're suppressing your true beliefs? If you have children, this area can be critical to the success of your relationship and to the religious philosophy of your children.

Lisa was Greek Orthodox and Dennis was Protestant. They didn't attend any particular church, but when they married, Lisa's church had them sign a paper that they would raise their children Greek Orthodox. They had their first son baptized Greek Orthodox at three months and raised him under that congregation until the age of ten. They did the same for their second son. Raising their children Greek Orthodox wasn't a problem for Lisa's husband because he didn't go to his church. Once their children were teenagers, Lisa and Dennis allowed their sons to make their own decisions about religious choice. One child converted to Episcopalian, then converted to Roman Catholic. Their other son changed his religious preference to Methodist.

Depending on the strength of their convictions, some parents are adamant about what religion they will raise their children. Since Lisa's husband didn't actively participate in any particular religion and she wanted her children to have a choice in their personal spiritual beliefs, the children may not have felt a strong attachment to their Greek Orthodox upbringing.

Which religious preference and the spiritual foundation you raise your children under is a very personal choice. If you and your partner have different faiths, you should discuss and decide in which faith you will raise your children before you even get pregnant. If your extended family has strong feelings on this subject, impress upon them the need to respect your decision and absolutely not to take out their disagreement on your child or children or spouse.

Fertility

Many women today are postponing pregnancy until after they have established a career, and they often find themselves in their mid-thirties to early forties before having their first child. Although you may feel this is the optimal time to have a baby, becoming pregnant after age thirty-five places you and your baby at higher risk for complications.

For women, statistics indicate that the safest and best time to have a baby is between the ages of twenty and thirty-five.[3] Earlier than that, the bones and ligaments of a woman's pelvis may not be ready to support a pregnancy. There is also a higher risk of complications with premature babies and full-term underweight babies because teenagers' eating habits are not always suitable for pregnancy.

After the age of thirty-five, women's eggs become less potent and getting pregnant may be more difficult. In addition, the possibility of having a baby with chromosomal defects increases significantly. Often, older women who experience difficulty in getting pregnant will seek out infertility specialists for assistance. In most cases, treating infertility is not covered under insurance and can be quite expensive. But when a couple is determined to have a baby, concern over cost often seems to go out the window. Therefore, if you know that you want a baby, for health and cost reasons you may want to start thinking about getting pregnant before your thirty-fifth birthday.

Values

Another area that you may want to explore with your partner is a comparison of your respective values. What do you consider worthwhile—family, friends, relationships, health, education, tradition? Do you share the same money values? Do your family values include children in your future? If your partner's views on children are not the same as yours, ask yourself again if these differences can be overcome. Are you willing to invest the time to work out your differences?

Remember, personal values and beliefs are developed from childhood through adulthood. They are deeply seated in an individual's character and are emotionally attached to identity. It can take a long time for couples with differing views and perspectives to relate to and understand each other. Often, people feel threatened if another person is trying to change their perception on a particular value. Add differing values on children to the equation and fireworks may occur. Not handled properly, conflict in any of your values and beliefs can cause emotions to escalate, making it difficult to communicate viewpoints rationally.

Take the time to sit down and calmly discuss with your partner all of the potential issues that can arise from having a child. Your relationship is worth it; invest your time wisely and work on one problem area at a time.

Chapter 3

Setting the Ground Rules

As a couple, you need to discover what type of communication works best. Having opposing views on children is not an easy situation for any couple to address. This is a life-altering decision, and chances are that if you're reading this, you can relate to the magnitude of this dilemma. Due to the sensitivity of this subject, many couples feel frustratingly isolated as they try to deal with this problem on their own.

The decision-making process can be difficult and often painful, but the rewards in having a stronger, more loving relationship far outweigh the consequences of not trying to communicate at all. When preparing to discuss a topic of this magnitude, you should first propose an agenda and set ground rules for discussions to prevent an emotionally charged discussion from escalating out of control. This will help both of you realize that working through the conflict together, or with outside help, will enhance and strengthen your relationship.

Change Your Environment

Where you have your discussions can profoundly affect the success or downfall of reaching a resolution on children. To keep things fresh, you may want periodically to change the location in which you discuss your differing perspectives. For example, if you always choose to talk about your issues while sitting on the couch or at the dining table, you and your partner may feel compelled to work on your "problem" every time the two of you are present in these locations. As time passes, a negative feeling may become associated with some of your favorite areas, and you or your partner may find yourselves avoiding those rooms. For this reason, it is important to change locations from time to time.

Choose neutral environments in your home by selecting the front room for one session, the home office for the next session, the dining room for the following session, and so on. Mix it up by feeding the pigeons in the park (avoid the children's play area for obvious reasons). Don't have discussions at your parents' house or at the in-laws'—especially if they have feelings about the situation. Also, the bedroom should be off-limits for this discussion—although agreements can be celebrated there. The bedroom should be reserved for intimate moments; having discussions of this type could tarnish the intimacy of the room. Remember, changing your environment for discussion purposes can give a fresh perspective on the issue.

If you already have children and are considering more, try to arrange for a sitter and go out, or have someone take the kids out for an adventure while you and your partner have a discussion. Your child could easily misinterpret emotions she overhears, you could be interrupted, and of course any successes can be better celebrated in privacy.

You may want to make an agreement on when to talk about your differences. Discussing serious issues late at night, when fatigued, can be difficult. Be aware of the hour and try to target your conversations at an optimal hour when both of you will feel alert. Discussing your problems in various locations, when both of you are attentive, can create a more relaxed, healthful home environment for you and your partner.

During your talks, avoid alcohol, turn off televisions and cell phones to prevent distractions, and keep the location relatively private. The intent is to provide a calm, nonthreatening environment where a serious discussion and life-altering agreement(s) can occur. Both of you should be alert, rested, and not agitated.

Say What You Want

Rule number one: Do not assume. Your partner is not a mind reader. Unless you tell him, he will not know your needs and desires.

Prior to my marriage to Ken, we had only spoken briefly about our thoughts on children, and I assumed Ken would get a reverse vasectomy. My comments about having children were pushed aside in pursuit of other goals. Instead of confronting Ken with my true feelings, I let things fester inside myself. It wasn't until I turned forty that I was straightforward with Ken and told him that I wanted a baby. Until that time, Ken had no idea how strongly I felt about wanting to have children, and I didn't realize how much he didn't want them.

By telling your partner what you want, you immediately identify conflict, and this provides an opportunity to learn about your partner, about yourself, and about the relationship.

State the Reasons for Your Desires

Before you can ascertain the reasons you want certain things in life, you first must determine if:

+ You want to have children.
+ You don't want to have children.
+ You want to wait to have children.
+ You're not sure yet and need time to decide.

If you are undecided and need additional time, or decide to wait to have children, establish the length of time, in months or years, or an event that needs to occur first. This way, it will be clear how long you will postpone parenthood or make a decision one way or the other. If your biological clock is ticking away, further delay of a hoped-for family may not be a good choice. It's easy to get caught up in the stressors of life and continue to delay starting a family. In our lifetimes, most of us will experience job changes, large-item purchases that throw us into debt, serious illnesses in the family, and the deaths of loved ones—all of these factors can prolong your decision to have children. If this is the case, take a close look at why you're putting off your decision. Ask yourself if these "life stressors" are excuses for not having children at all. To ensure consensus on the amount of time you've planned to wait, you may want to address this subject periodically.

Share the Problem Equally

If you're a couple, the decision to have a child or to remain childless is a joint decision. If a child is brought into a relationship in which one partner is opposed to having a baby, the relationship will usually suffer, and as a result so does the child. On the other hand, making the decision to remain childless only to appease one partner can cause built-up resentment and anger, placing a heavy burden on the relationship. Early in your discussions, you need to realize the importance of working on this problem as a couple; approaching it as "ours." This decision affects both of you. For the health and preservation of your relationship, it's important that you share this problem as a team and approach it with the utmost honesty.

Actively Listen to Each Other

Acknowledge what your partner says and listen with empathy. Take notes if necessary. You might misinterpret what your partner is saying or means to say. If you're not certain you understood what he said, rephrase what you heard in your own words. For example, begin with, "So, what I heard you say was . . . " and then state what you heard. After that, ask the question, "Did I have the right understanding?" instead of saying, "You can't be serious!" My husband and I used this technique and found it to be beneficial. Rephrasing what you heard is a nonthreatening way to clarify what was said. In most cases, it increases the level of understanding for both parties and allows communication to flow more freely. Active listening can also help increase the level of compassion.

Remain Calm and Take Frequent Breaks

This is an emotional issue and tempers may flare on occasion. Recognize this in advance and plan accordingly. Taking breaks gives each of you the opportunity to reflect and consider each other's perspective. Conflicting views on the subject of children can cause emotions to intensify and often creates anxiety. People confronting this issue will feel threatened or fearful, which can put them on the defensive. A resentful partner can cause anger, bitter feelings, further resentment, and heated arguments that can stifle progress and severely affect the relationship. This is why it's important to think carefully about how you will phrase your comments and questions. Opposing views on children are a delicate conversation area. Remaining calm requires discipline and self-control.

If you do find yourself in a situation in which your partner is raising his voice, remain calm and let him vent. This helps diffuse anger and allows your partner to express himself. If the situation gets out of control, acknowledge your partner's viewpoint, take a break, and come back to the subject later when you are fresh.

By remaining calm, your mind is clearer, and it's easier to communicate your thoughts logically in a way that your partner might be more receptive to. It also creates a more favorable environment for open communication.

Be Open to Each Other's Point of View

Have compassion for your partner—you're in love . . . remember? Remain nonjudgmental by listening to his side and by putting yourself in his shoes. One way to do this is to be objective. Let your partner explain his perceptions of having children so you can relate to his side of the equation with empathy. Then, explain why you feel the way you do about children. Be open and honest. Where there is truth, there is strength.

Review Childhood Experiences

Tell each other more about your childhood. Disclosing certain events in your childhood can reveal facts about what has affected the way you feel about children today. For example, if your parents divorced when you were a child, the breakup of the family may affect your outlook on having children of your own. In most cases, talking about your childhood sheds light into a hidden area that allows for greater understanding. Long-term effects of generations of families, of parents' and grandparents' influence, are enormous whether you realize it or not. Some childhood-related questions you may want to consider asking include:

How did you see your parents communicate with each other?
How did they solve problems?
How did they make decisions?

The answers to these questions will help each of you understand how the other communicates and why.

After you and your partner have discussed your childhoods, explain why it's so important for you to have children or why it's so important for you to remain childless. As you do so, remain calm and impartial. There are no right or wrong answers here; you are simply stating your views. Ideally, writing each of your positions on a sheet of paper, then reviewing and rewriting your thoughts, allows each of you to clarify and reach a better understanding of the other's point of view. This will do much to facilitate openness between you.

Identify Each Other's Desires

Figure out how children may or may not affect your and your partner's desires and interests. For example, how would this affect your career, your expenses, your vacations, your savings, your retirement? Do you share the same thoughts on parenting, discipline, and education? Have you identified the costs of having a child, such as medical insurance, hospital expenses, child care, baby furniture, clothing, and college? These are all legitimate questions that will be affected by your decision to have children or to remain child-free. This process can be helpful in developing your decision. Having read Chapter 2, you have already done some thinking on these issues, and now it is time for your partner to do the same.

Stay Focused

It's easy to get sidetracked. Stick to the facts and the issue at hand: the decision to have or not to have children. It's easy to become distracted with other topics. If you find yourselves on a different subject, acknowledge the fact, ask if you can get back to it another time, and set a time, and then when the time comes, refocus your conversation back to where it was before you got sidetracked. By doing this, you'll be able to refocus without negating the other subject and possibly hurting your partner's feelings. Help each other by redirecting the conversation when you stray. Staying focused takes teamwork. This is an emotional issue, and digressions are likely and could be deliberate to avoid confrontation. Remember that your goal is to reach a mutually satisfying agreement about children and, through the process, to build and strengthen your relationship.

Take Things Slowly

Achieving consensus takes time. Be prepared to take things slowly. Initially discuss your problem no more than twice a week. Some couples may feel comfortable talking about their differences on children once every one or two weeks and occasionally may allow three weeks to elapse before talking about children again. During each session, try to work on your decision-making problem for at least an hour. If you find your conversation getting too intense, take a break and come back to the topic later. Many couples find that taking time out and discussing their problem at a later date works well. For this reason, we recommend that you take a breather when you find things getting heated. Make a point to get back to the issue, but don't shelve it for too long.

Dr. John Gottman, coauthor of *The Seven Principles for Making Marriage Work*, holds that if the problem is a "present" problem—one that is current with no links to the past—then it is usually a solvable problem. Solvable problems are much easier to resolve than perpetual problems, which include those connected to the past.[1] With perpetual problems, the couple seems to get stuck and keeps repeating the issue with no resolution. Often, people with differing views on children will find themselves stuck in a perpetual problem due to their childhood experiences. Until the person with the problem can identify and resolve the issue hooked to the past, his subconscious will prevent him from progressing. You can see that this can be an exhausting process until addressed properly.

Consider a different approach for your next session. Review what went well in previous talks and build on that. Learn from what didn't go well and try not to repeat that situation again. Keep working on your decision to have children or to remain child-free until you have reached a resolution that both of you are comfortable with.

Plan a Target Date

When do you want to come to an agreement on children or when do you want to evaluate your progress? Be clear on the purpose of the target date: evaluation or agreement. Everyone is different, and depending on your circumstances, you might find yourselves reaching an amicable agreement in a relatively short period or it may take you longer than you anticipated.

Since this is a highly charged emotional area, consensus can take time. My husband and I took eight months to reach a mutual decision to have children. For some people, eight months is a relatively short period to arrive at a conclusion on a decision of this magnitude. For others who hear their biological clock ticking away, eight months can seem a lifetime to resolve this problem. Regardless of the length of time you spend, the resolution process takes full commitment from both parties. It's not something you can work on for a month and then push aside for two years or more.

Don't be too aggressive and, if the situation warrants it, be flexible, patient, and understanding. If necessary, extend the target date or seek outside help through third-party counseling.

Keep Family and Friends Out of It

When it comes to your well-being, it can be extremely difficult for your family and friends to be objective. For most of you, your family has known you all your life and, in most cases, they love you very much and want the best for you. This includes your happiness. If you're upset and confide in them about a problem you're having with your partner, it's only natural for your family to focus on your sadness and to take your side. Many of your friends may react in the same way. When this happens, you open your partner up for attack, which can cause additional stress and problems in your relationship. This is not what you want.

Your family and friends' negative reactions toward your partner when you share this information can create anxiety. For this reason, many couples decide to work on their problem privately as a team or seek outside help through counseling.

If you do decide to confide in your family or friends on this issue, be prepared for the fact that they might support you but not your relationship with your partner.

Be Honest with Yourself

A decision of this magnitude must come from the heart. If the decision to have a child is made only to appease you, there is a danger that after the child is born, your partner will harbor built-up resentment toward you and possibly the child. As a result, he might distance himself from the family through distractions of work or other activities. As the years pass, perhaps five or ten years down the road, his internal anger may surface in frequent arguments. At that point, he might argue about different problems, not relating them to the true foundation of his anger. You and your partner might think you had already worked out your opposing desires to have children; and in reality, you had not. In this case, there is high probability that your relationship will suffer as will, perhaps, the stability of your child.

This scenario is also possible for those who decide to remain childless to appease their partner. If this is the case, you're not only lying to yourself, you're lying to your partner. This breaks the trust in the relationship. If your decision doesn't come from your heart, you run the risk of harboring built-up resentment toward your partner, which can lead to separation or divorce. Remember, regardless of your decision, it is best to be true to yourself.

Setting ground rules will greatly assist you and your partner as you venture through this tumultuous time together resolving your differences. Follow the guidelines outlined in this chapter:

1. Change your environment.
2. Say what you want.
3. State the reasons for your desires.
4. Share the problem equally.
5. Actively listen to each other.
6. Remain calm and take frequent breaks.
7. Be open to each other's point of view.
8. Review childhood experiences.
9. Identify each other's desires.
10. Stay focused.
11. Take things slowly.
12. Plan a target date.
13. Keep family and friends out of it.
14. Be honest with yourself.

Until you resolve this conflict, the problem will lurk beneath the surface of your relationship. When that happens, it may manifest in hidden resentment, which will escalate into expressed anger toward your partner or lead to stagnation, separation, or divorce. This is not the goal. The goal is to salvage your relationship and strengthen your love for each other while reaching a decision about children—a decision that is equally shared in your hearts.

Part II

Dealing with the Conflict

Chapter 4

Overcoming Fears

For many men, being asked to become a father can be a fearful proposition. These fears—sometimes legitimate and sometimes less so—are obstacles that need to be addressed if he is to change his mind about becoming a father, and if the marriage is to be fulfilling. Why might men be fearful about becoming fathers? The National Fatherhood Initiative offers these fatherly facts, which may substantiate your partner's fears[1]:

+ Thirty-four percent of children, or 24 million children, do not live in the same house as their biological father.
+ The divorce rate of first marriages within fifteen years is 43 percent; nearly 60 percent of those divorcing have children; and about 1 million children experience the divorce of their parents each year.
+ There are more than 3.3 million children who live with an unwed parent and his/her live-in partner. Census supports that the

number of cohabitating couples with children has almost doubled since 1990 to 1.7 million today.

+ Twenty-six percent of biological fathers live in a different state than their children; around 40 percent of children whose fathers don't live in the home have not seen their father in more than a year; and half of children in absent-father homes have never been to their father's home.

+ Statistics indicate that, on average, children who live in a home without their biological father present are two to three times more likely to experience health, educational, emotional, and behavioral problems; to use drugs; to be poor; to be victims of child abuse; and to be involved in criminal behavior than children who live with biological or adoptive married parents.

These facts alone will scare a lot of men into not wanting to have children. As mentioned in Chapter 1, if people have not resolved issues experienced during their childhood, they often repeat those experiences in marital relationships. Dr. Kovacs has discovered that one of the reasons adolescence is so stressful is because one or both parents start to relive their own adolescent conflicts or issues, which may be similar to their child's conflict/issue. The pattern is repeated until the issue is resolved.

Tim's parents divorced when he was seven years old, which deeply impacted his thoughts on children. When he and Julie first married, Julie agreed not to have children. Five years into the marriage, at age thirty-seven, Julie's maternal instincts kicked in like a sonic boom that jolted Tim out of his seat (see page 19). He had told Julie from the beginning that he didn't want children, and he didn't want to discuss the subject when she tried to bring it up. But Julie needed to envision and plan for their lives over the next ten to twenty years, so she needed to talk about their future, with or without children. During one of Julie's attempts to discuss their situation, Tim actually said, "I'm not having children until my parents get back together!" Julie sat back a little surprised and said, "Now, that's a profound statement."

That statement certainly was insightful because Tim's parents had divorced thirty-one years earlier; he was now thirty-eight, and the odds that his parents would reunite were dismal. Because of Tim's painful experience with the divorce of his parents, he strongly felt that children meant pain and that children were the root cause of a marriage's deteriorating to the point of divorce. Tim felt that he was the reason his parents had divorced—he felt responsible. For thirty-one years, he had been carrying around the heavy burden of guilt, blame, rejection, loss, and pain. Tim felt the best way to protect himself from experiencing those emotions again was never to have children and perpetuate his experience with the next generation.

What Worked:

+ Tim's admission that he wasn't going to have children until his parents got back together was a startling realization for him. Both he and Julie quickly recognized that he needed to resolve this issue before they could progress with their decision to have children.
+ They also realized that they were not equipped to handle a situation like this on their own.
+ While they researched a therapist to assist them, Julie also suggested that Tim talk to his friends who were already fathers.
+ One of Tim's male friends took him aside and angrily stated, "Who are you to deny your wife children?" That statement alone startled Tim, and he decided to take a good long look at himself. This only confirmed that he was right to seek out counseling.
+ Tim was pleasantly surprised and relieved to hear that his male friends adored and loved their children. More than one of his friends said, "Children don't prevent you from doing things; you just have a different way of doing them." Tim observed that children did not change his friends' personalities—they survived, and he could too.
+ Julie and Tim selected a therapist who saw them separately. After resolving Tim's issue with his parents' divorce, the therapist saw

Tim and Julie together to work on their decision about whether to have a child. Trying to resolve their stalemate on children would have been fruitless without first working on Tim's childhood experiences with his parents' separation and divorce.

+ During Tim's sessions, the therapist assisted him in overcoming the sadness and disappointment about his parents' divorce. This enabled Tim to begin the healing process and to forgive his parents for their decision to end their relationship.

What Didn't Work:
+ For Julie and Tim, what didn't work was no discussion at all.
+ Julie's insistence on having children was not helping the situation.
+ Tim was trying to resolve his feelings about his parents' divorce himself, without professional counseling.
+ The two first tried to work on their conflict without outside counseling. Fortunately, Julie and Tim recognized early on that they needed assistance and took action.

Analysis

Julie and Tim were keenly aware that they had a problem and shared equally in the responsibility to resolve their issue. Tim showed courage and a deep trust in his relationship with Julie when he told his innermost feelings to her and to a therapist. Five years into the marriage, when her biological clock sounded, Julie acknowledged that she had changed her mind about having children and was honest about her feelings. Tim sought out advice from male friends, which eased his fears and also motivated him to examine his core beliefs and issues about children. Julie and Tim were also careful in their selection of the right therapist, were sincere in their sessions, and were rewarded with a mutual agreement to have children.

Once Tim realized that he was not the cause for his parents' divorce, he was able to move forward to explore his true feelings about starting a family with his wife. Julie and Tim decided to have a baby. This experience transformed Tim into a caring, supportive, loving father. He was there in the delivery room, cut the umbilical cord, and from the time their son came home, Tim has shared equally in the daily care and raising of their son. Julie and Tim's son is now four years old, and Tim says of fatherhood, "The experience of being a father has far exceeded any expectations I had previously. Having children has been an enormously rewarding pleasure."

If Tim has truly resolved his issue with his parents' divorce, then he and Julie will have a greater chance of dealing effectively with other problems when they arise. If not, then a reworking of the residual issue may be necessary for a short period. The critical time for Tim's marriage will come when his son turns seven, because that is the age at which Tim's parents divorced.

Men who have experienced a similar issue, whose parents divorced while they were children, may need outside help in moving forward in their lives. Since the subject of children and divorce is a delicate and painful matter, people should seek professional help and not try to resolve this issue alone.

What if a partner's parents were happily married throughout his childhood, yet he still has fears of parenthood? Jim was fearful of becoming a father, even though he felt his own father did a good job of raising him. His dad worked hard, kept the kids in line with the threat of spankings, and took the family on summer vacations. There were lots of family events with aunts and uncles and grandparents.

Jim had married and divorced within three years, without having any children. He was so fearful of being a poor dad that he got a vasectomy to prevent any possibility. Then Jim met Sharon. He told her about his vasectomy, and they fell in love, married, and—you guessed it—Sharon wanted children. Through many discussions, often late at night, Sharon discovered that Jim thought he would not make a good father because he felt inadequate in disciplining and he also thought he wouldn't have time for children. His experiences with children were mostly negative—the screaming kids at the supermarket checkout line, and inevitably on flights, the kid in the seat behind him with the hyperactive feet.

Each of these episodes convinced Jim that he lacked the patience for children and that kids, in fact, drove him nuts.

Jim had been raised in an emotionally conservative family, with few demonstrations of love or any outward signs of affection for one another. He was the middle child, with an older brother and a younger sister, each spaced a few years apart. With such a large age range between siblings, their interests varied widely. As a result, Jim developed a sense of independence at a young age. He never had trouble entertaining himself and seldom felt lonely. Although Jim didn't spend a lot of time with his older brother, his observation of his older brother's experience—breaking curfew, picking fights, and general misbehaving—taught Jim what not to do.

Jim knew his parents were always there for him, and although they loved and provided well for Jim and his siblings, the closeness that he desired and had seen in other families (and on TV) wasn't expressed openly. His family didn't hug a lot or show affection, but he became an affectionate person nonetheless.

Jim had been elated when Sharon came into his life, but he had no strong desire to add children into their "perfect" lives. The couple worked on their disagreements together as a team. Jim allowed Sharon to express why it was so important for her to have a child. In turn, she listened to all his reasons for not wanting to have children. They empathized with each other, they disclosed their childhoods to each other, and they had a greater understanding of the other's needs. They talked with other couples that had gone through the same conflict on children. They also sought out counseling, and persevered with their relationship, trying to conclude an amicable agreement on children.

To ease Jim's fear of a vasectomy reversal, Sharon found another couple that had gone through the process and shared their experiences from it.

Jim also talked to male friends about their experiences of being a father. Each said that having children was a joy, that the first two years were the most incredible because a child changes and develops so much over such a short period. The more these men talked about their children, the more animated they became. Jim was completely immersed in what these men had to say about being dads. He was seeing and hearing that men could truly be happy with children. Talking with men about their experience of being a father assisted Jim in developing a new perspective of fatherhood.

What Worked:

+ Jim and Sharon approached their conflict on children as a team. They openly listened to each other, expressed their views, and empathized with each other.

+ They talked about their childhood experiences and how that influenced their feelings on children. Listening to Jim tell about his childhood helped Sharon better understand him and why he felt the way he did.

+ Jim and Sharon talked with other couples with similar experiences, and Jim talked to his male friends, who gave him a more positive feeling toward fatherhood.

+ They continued to work on their differences until they resolved their conflict.

What Didn't Work:

+ What didn't work for Jim and Sharon was trying to work on their problem late at night when they were both tired. Jim also felt that the subject intruded into the bedroom—their intimate place.

+ When they realized they needed outside help, they chose a counselor, but Jim didn't find the sessions helpful, and he and Sharon quickly thought that they could do better working out the issue on their own.

+ Their visit with another "postvasectomy-reversal happy couple" wasn't completely positive either. Jim thought they were a nice couple with cute kids, but the two things he remembered the most about the visit were the gory details of the reversal and the fact that the husband never talked to his wife and only focused on the kids. The last thing Jim wanted out of his decision to have children was to distance himself from Sharon.

Analysis

Sharon and Jim tried a variety of methods to resolve their differing opinions on children and continued to work through their issues. Due to Jim's vasectomy, their decision-making was more involved than for another couple. Additionally, Jim had issues with his fear of losing independence—in his life and in his relationship.

Having children of his own would mean he wouldn't experience the same level of independence he had enjoyed since his childhood, but he would experience the perceived miseries of parenthood from his most remembered scenes between his parents. He also thought—again from observing his parents—that children didn't allow a husband and wife to be close anymore. This was not something that Jim wanted to happen. By associating Jim's experiences from his parents' relationship with how he felt about children, Sharon had a better understanding of why he didn't want children. Still, she felt as strongly about wanting children as she did before.

What really changed Jim's mind was realizing the strength of his relationship with Sharon and wanting to keep it strong. He also felt a lot of pain when he saw Sharon going through emotional turbulence. With this in mind, Jim realized that it was okay for him to be open to the possibility of children in their lives.

Their journey wasn't always easy, and sometimes the paths they took to assist in their decision-making process didn't quite work out, but they hung in there as a couple until they reached a mutually satisfying agreement.

Borrowing Kids

Taking care of your niece or nephew or a good friend's child does not evoke the same feelings as raising your own children. In addition, taking care of young children between the ages of two and five can be very difficult at times and may not give your partner the best experience or impression of what to anticipate in parenthood. Many parents have said that taking care of nieces and nephews is nothing like bringing home your own newborn. The bond is different; the love is different. There's no comparison. If you insist on exposing your partner to babysitting, here's a cautionary tale.

To give Ken a better experience with children, I decided that a weekend with my nephew and niece would be a great break for my brother and sister-in-law and a chance for Ken to experience a wonderful weekend with children. They arrived on Friday night with excitement in their eyes and high-fives all around. To make the evening kid-friendly, I planned to ask Ken and the kids to pick up a pizza, then we would watch a Disney video and put the kids to bed when they fell asleep. Saturday, we would spend the day feeding the ducks by a nearby pond, take naps in the afternoon, and enjoy a chicken dinner with corn on the cob.

From Ken's perspective, here's what actually happened (those of you who are already parents out there can chuckle all you want):

+ As soon as their mother left the apartment, the youngest began to cry . . . and cry, and cry.
+ The trip to the pizza parlor resulted in a Marx Brothers–like scene with the kids emptying salt and pepper shakers, throwing napkins into the air, and the owner requesting that they never set foot in his place again.
+ The kids were not ready for bed at the end of the *Lion King*, but the babysitters were.
+ On Saturday, Donna realized she needed more corn and sent Ken and the youngest to the store. Once in his car seat, the child started screaming in the back of the car, in the shopping cart seat (that raised a lot of eyebrows in the parking lot!), and all the way home, ending thirty seconds prior to entering the apartment.

What Worked:
+ The parents had a great weekend in the mountains.
+ Planning kid-friendly activities prior to the visit definitely helped.

What Didn't Work:

+ Taking care of a two-year-old and a five-year-old for their first overnight visit away from their parents provided a recipe for disaster.
+ Taking care of more than one child at a time was too much for nonparents to handle.
+ Sending Ken on an errand with two children alone wasn't fair to Ken or the kids.

Analysis

My heart was in the right place, but perhaps we should have agreed to taking care of one child at a time. Two children, away from home for the first time, with inexperienced babysitters—we were destined for failure and aspirin. My idea to have Ken go to the pizza parlor would have worked if there had been only one child. Two can feed off each other, especially if they have not been exposed to a disciplined environment outside their own home. To have this concept work, a child with a preschool experience or one who has already experienced a fun night away from home would have been a better choice. Or even taking care of an infant for ten to fifteen minutes in their home would be another alternative.

Kid-friendly food was a smart move as was a trip to the pond to feed the ducks. As for the trip to the supermarket, checkout areas with all of the loose candy bars tax even the most experienced mother's patience. Someone with Ken's preconceived notions of children wouldn't stand a chance. Unfortunately this experience in "practice parenting" did not work out in our favor.

For Ken, the entire experience was a nightmare. As mentioned earlier, nephews and nieces are not substitutes for the real thing, especially when they are young and away from home for the first time. Add to this the fact that they were two young, energetic, and mischievous children, and you have the makings of a weekend that reinforced virtually every stereotype Ken had about children. This "practice parenting" experience did more damage than good and working through the issue took weeks to repair. Oh, and Ken is still banned from the pizza parlor—six years later.

Each couple is different and each situation involving fear of becoming a parent is unique. The biggest hurdle is to recognize that the fear may be stemming from an unresolved issue from childhood. Adults need to review their childhood and their perceptions of their parents as husband and wife. Ongoing communication on a regular basis, perhaps two to three times a week, with attentive listening and validation of each other's statements, feelings, and concerns will assist in resolving conflict in this area. When stuck, consult with a professional marriage and family therapist who can assist you.

Follow the examples of the two couples in this chapter: Be honest with your feelings, wants, and desires; review your childhoods and how that has affected your thoughts on children; empathize with each other; avoid late-night discussions; talk with friends who are parents; and if the fears cannot be overcome, seek out a therapist.

For the partner who is considering becoming a father: Settle your fears so you don't repeat past experiences, and then be prepared for your new responsibilities and for one of the most fascinating, rewarding times of your life.

When He's Not Saying "No" but "Not Yet"

Prior to the 1960s, people who got married were essentially committed to starting a family. You fell in love, he had a good job, your father didn't dislike him too much, you got married and shortly afterward had a baby. The introduction and common use of birth control in the 1960s changed this scenario drastically. Couples began to have the option to delay having children until fully ready, both emotionally and financially. This revolutionary change in our society has resulted in more couples, one or both partners, deciding not only to delay childbirth, but also to delay making the decision of when or if to have children.

Although couples have taken control of their family choices, sometimes the male partner continues to delay when to begin the family—he's not saying no, but he is saying, "Not Yet." Now comes the need for a couple to set conditions for *when*. For instance, many couples want to build their careers and increase their incomes before starting a family. This is especially true when the mother wants to stay home to raise children while her partner is the primary provider. But postponing children to build a career may take longer than a woman wants to wait.

Sometimes couples defer one goal to accelerate the attainment of another. Saving to purchase a new car may delay paying off a student loan, going on that vacation of a lifetime may delay the purchase of a house, or saving to buy a house may delay the start of a family. Other times, a former high-priority goal of having children is moved to a lower priority when a couple encounters an unforeseen obstacle such as the loss of a job or a sudden disability. In these cases, it may be more acceptable to both partners to postpone children. Regardless, it is important to the success of the relationship that the couple agrees on their goals.

Many people reprioritize their goals depending on emotional or physical needs. In today's world, people are inundated with advertising that promotes impulse buying. Often people make purchases based on emotion, not realizing at the time that they may be sacrificing another goal. These impulse buys can substantially impact the financial goals that you agreed on for the timing of having children. (Did you really need to purchase that state-of-the-art flat-panel entertainment center with surround sound?) As a couple, you need to be conscious of changes to your goals and how they will impact your family planning objectives. When the timing continues to remain unresolved in spite of achievement of your set conditions, or if new conditions have been introduced, this may give the impression that one partner is indirectly saying no to children. When the timing continues to shift, this issue becomes "perpetual" and needs to be addressed accordingly.

Dr. John Gottman, a leading research scientist and writer on marriage and family issues, has classified all marital conflicts into two categories: those that can be resolved and those that are perpetual.[1] A perpetual problem is one that doesn't go away with time. In stable relationships, many couples deal with perpetual problems by joking about the situation because they know they will never agree and they accept their problem as is. However, in unstable relationships, perpetual problems can be damaging. Children often fit into the perpetual problem, and certainly the decision whether to have a baby would fit into the perpetual problem if left unresolved.

This was the case for Deborah and Michael (introduced on page 8). Early in their relationship, Deborah and Michael were equally open to children. Both were in their late twenties, but Deborah was concerned about her ability to conceive because her older sister had difficulty getting pregnant. Unconcerned, Michael wanted to postpone children—and he assured Deborah he was still very much interested in having them—until after they purchased a house. Deborah again relayed her fear that it may take them a few years to get pregnant. In addition, she thought that getting pregnant would not make an impact on their expenses. She thought they could still achieve their goal of becoming homeowners and start a family at the same time. Still, Michael convinced Deborah they should wait until after they'd purchased a house.

After moving into their new home, Deborah again approached Michael about starting a family. He explained that he wanted Deborah to be able to stay home to raise their children. He was up for a promotion and wanted to wait for the results. Michael got the promotion, but when Deborah wanted to celebrate by starting a family, Michael said he wanted to wait another four to six months to establish himself in his new position before they attempted to get pregnant. Deborah understood, but at the same time she felt this was another excuse not to start a family . . . yet.

Deborah was suppressing her anger and holding on to resentment toward her husband for not allowing her to have the family of her dreams. Michael continued to raise excuse after excuse to postpone children, and although Deborah very much wanted to start a family, she always gave in to her husband's requests. This went on for a number of years. Deborah is now thirty-nine and certain that she will never fulfill her dream of having children.

What Worked:
+ The fact that Deborah and Michael identified early in their relationship that they wanted children was beneficial.

+ Agreeing to start a family at the completion of a goal motivated Deborah.

What Didn't Work:

+ Michael's perpetual postponement by adding another goal before starting a family went on for more than ten years.
+ Both had valid reasons for wanting to postpone and wanting to start a family, but they didn't clearly addressed their wants and goals and what was causing them to get stuck.
+ They did not set a firm timeline for when they would start a family.
+ Deborah suppressed her true feelings about her goal for when she wanted to start a family and reluctantly agreed to support Michael's goals.
+ They did not look into possible fertility issues with a specialist and how that would affect their ability to have children, especially when Deborah reached thirty-five.

Analysis

Deborah and Michael's delay was a perpetual problem. Deborah believed that her needs and goals to have a family were being rejected, and she didn't acknowledge her anger or her feelings of rejection. Instead she suppressed her feelings and complied with Michael's new goals each time. Michael also didn't acknowledge his reasons for wanting to postpone fatherhood. As long as Deborah complied, Michael continued to postpone having a child. Apparently, both had unresolved issues, which probably had family-of-origin patterns. Even though they continue to talk about when they will have children, they never make headway by committing to that goal. As a result, Deborah continues to feel frustrated, hurt, and angry, and neither is willing to confront the underlying obstacles.

Although Deborah and Michael initially agreed to have children and set criteria for when they would start trying, they still needed to take their planning a step farther. They needed to be motivated to explore any hidden issues preventing them from moving forward. This can be frightening and it takes understanding by both parties. Why was Michael always delaying when they would start a family? Were the additional goals a distraction from the real reason he didn't want to start a family? Why did Deborah continue to appease her husband? Did she secretly have reservations about having children?

When Michael continuously delayed, it appeared he really meant no to children all together. If this was the case, he was not being truthful about wanting to start a family. What was Michael conveying to Deborah? First, he wanted a home; then he was also giving her the impression that they would raise their family someday and that he wanted to support them with his income. He wanted Deborah to stay at home and raise their children with their values, and he was not worried about her possible infertility problem. This was an ideal situation for any couple. Deborah, on the other hand, was concerned about postponing a family for fear of missing out on the opportunity to have children, but she did not express her concerns.

Instead, Michael kept replacing one attained goal with another, unrelated to children, and Deborah continued to comply with his wishes. Deborah's goal of having a family was continually dismissed, seemingly with her approval, which was resulting in a buildup of resentment toward her husband. Her dream was not being fulfilled. This couple was clearly avoiding the problem year after year. There were obvious communication disconnections. Compromises were made that only supported a win/lose situation, and Deborah was on the losing end throughout their discussions. In addition, Deborah and Michael needed to understand the infertility issues that ran in Deborah's family and how they might impact their ability to have children.

According to Dr. Gottman's system for resolving perpetual problems, Michael and Deborah will need motivation and willingness to explore the hidden issues that are blocking them from progressing in achieving their goal. If they are unable to share with each other their dreams about children and what they mean to each of them, then reaching out for assistance from a therapist is the next step to take.

Stating the reasons for your desire to have children and what you envision your life to be like when you have children allows your partner to relate to your goals. This involves equal time, acceptance, and respect for your partner's goals. The discussion needs to be carried out in a calm, nonthreatening manner. If you're angry, postpone your conversation for another time because it will most likely end with a negative outcome. Dr. Gottman says that 96 percent of the time, the course of your conversation is determined by how you *begin* talking about issues.[2] If you start out angry, then the conversation has a high probability of escalating out of control. However, if you begin your talks on a more positive note, you are more likely to make headway and keep the conversation at an even level. Acknowledging each other's position on the issue is valuable in expressing understanding and empathy. Many couples' goals may be similar, but the individuals involved may not be on the same timeline. Talking with each other about your goals allows you to align your dreams for the future as a team and to set a target date. Couples who work together as a team to resolve their differences will be more successful than those who don't.

Elizabeth and Steve also found that they disagreed on when to have children. They met after college and married after a four-year courtship. While they were dating, they talked about their childhoods and discovered each had come from loving, family-oriented environments. This made each feel that the other would be a good parent because they had both come from stable homes. Talking about their childhoods also made them both feel more comfortable that the other would want to follow in the same path. Early in the relationship, it seemed they both had similar goals of having children. The timing issue didn't develop until four years later, just before their wedding.

As they got closer to marriage, Elizabeth mentioned that she wanted to start trying to get pregnant right away, but Steve wanted to wait. Elizabeth was concerned that she might have difficulty in getting pregnant at thirty. Steve wanted to wait until they were more financially stable. Elizabeth brought up the topic often, and they would sit down and discuss their differences on the timing of starting a family. They thought that talking about their positions helped by allowing each to know where the other was coming from.

During their discussions, they also uncovered some other areas of conflict that affected their decision. Because Elizabeth and Steve belonged to different religions, they had to determine in which religion they would raise a child. They also had opposing views on country versus city living. Elizabeth had been raised in the country, cherished her memories, and wanted their children to experience that type of lifestyle also. But Steve was raised in the city with more access to professional sporting events, museums, shopping malls, and more opportunities for career advancement. Each had a vision of what they perceived to be an ideal living environment, and in time they worked out their differences.

Their open communication intensified Elizabeth's desire for children and she felt more comfortable about Steve as a father. Elizabeth persisted with their discussions for a full year. In the end, although Steve wanted to wait longer, he agreed to start a family. They got pregnant right away. Elizabeth said that Steve didn't show excitement until seven months into the pregnancy. Once the baby was born, it was as if the timing had never been an issue.

Elizabeth said of the decision-making process, "Without a doubt, the open communication and learning more about one another was most rewarding. We worked on our differences and actually became closer." Asked about anything she would have done differently, she said, "I would have been more relaxed and not in as much of a hurry to get pregnant. I would have listened more about the financial issues. I still wouldn't have wanted to wait that much longer; however, looking back, I don't think either one of us has any regrets."

What Worked:
+ Elizabeth and Steve both had similar goals of having a family together.
+ They talked how about their childhoods influenced them.

+ Elizabeth frequently brought up the subject of when they would begin a family and the two communicated openly while reviewing their differences in a calm manner.
+ They extended their conversations to include environmental and religious preferences to raise their unborn children.

What Didn't Work:
+ Steve appeased his wife by reluctantly agreeing to start a family when he wasn't ready.
+ Steve did not express his thoughts or feelings until late in the pregnancy.

Analysis

Elizabeth and Steve's issue of "when" was a solvable problem. They were brave in tackling the topic until they reached a resolution. They persevered, due to Elizabeth's determination, and spoke often about when they would begin trying to get pregnant. Confronting an issue like this can be frightening for many couples. Some couples want to avoid confrontation on a sensitive subject out of fear of an argument. But, by not addressing the problem, the unresolved "issue" will, most likely, escalate into a much larger problem, or it may be suppressed and arise at a later time to disturb them.

This couple approached the subject in a nonthreatening, calm manner and stayed focused on their issue of "when." Again, when people approach an issue in a positive manner with a clear understanding of what they are trying to resolve, they are working as a team and have greater success in reaching a consensus. The key is to be specific about what you are trying to accomplish. By doing this, Elizabeth and Steve created an environment that allowed them greater communication and it also gave them an opportunity to learn more about each other. Communicating in this style strengthened their bond.

Steve and Elizabeth explored their childhoods, which gave them comfort about having children. Often if people have positive memories about their upbringing, they will be more inclined to want children of their own.

In addition, Elizabeth and Steve did not try to rush through their differences in order to reach an agreement. Their talks evolved into a compromise only after a full year of discussions and a decision that Steve still wasn't completely comfortable with. Often people will look for a quick solution to a problem. In their rush, they may not address the actual concern(s) of their partner. When that happens, the "solution" may be short-lived.

In Steve and Elizabeth's case, Steve was concerned about their financial strength while Elizabeth was concerned about her ability to become pregnant. After a year, Steve made a compromise to start a family under their current financial condition. This did not allow him the financial comfort level he wanted. As a result, when his wife immediately became pregnant, he did not show any outward signs of satisfaction until her seventh month of pregnancy. Elizabeth was keenly aware of Steve's emotions, which made her question if they were right to start a family. Fortunately, Steve was overjoyed at the birth of their baby and never mentioned the timing issue again. Ironically, Elizabeth later confessed that she wished they had been more financially stable at the time of her pregnancy. This couple learned that they were able to resolve their differences as a team by remaining calm and being specific about what they wanted.

Elizabeth and Steve actively listened to each other and acknowledged each other's views. If they continue to tackle future issues in this same manner, they will have a high probability of a successful marriage.

If you pay close attention to the issues your partner raises, at the time he raises them, then you will have more positive conversations. This shows respect for what your partner has to say. If you are having difficulty doing this, recall a time when you began your relationship—think of how attentively you listened and empathized with each other. This can assist in creating a mindset that will help you have better conversations.

A word of caution about making compromises: First, when you are making a compromise, know that you are essentially giving up something to gain agreement on something else. If you continuously insist on having your way, you are not going to have a great marriage. A great marriage evolves over time when, at key times in life, you put the needs of your relationship first and your individual wants second. Both parties perform a give and take. That's what compromise is all about.

What if you're a couple who has agreed to postpone children and you haven't addressed a timeline? Or, the two of you don't even know if you want to have children? If this describes your current marriage or relationship, you're most likely carrying on your lives together pursuing goals and enjoying your lifestyle, not wanting to address the subject until the maternal clock starts ticking furiously.

Mary and Todd met in college and dated for three years that were filled with summer and winter vacations and many family activities. They've now been married for four years, have purchased a house, and both are successful entrepreneurs with full schedules and a satisfying lifestyle. As for children, Mary says, "Todd and I have both been in agreement about putting off having a family. Over the past four years we've had plenty to occupy ourselves, but, because of my age, we will have to make a decision soon. I think we're both still on the fence about 'if' and 'when' to start a family. In all honesty, I wish I was about five years younger so that we wouldn't have to think about this for a while."

Analysis

With today's financial and social demands, Mary and Todd's situation of postponing children is becoming more commonplace. They both agreed to delay a family, which indicates one or both hope to have children at some point in their lives. At the same time, Mary has stated that they are still uncertain if they want to have children. To ensure that they are on the same page with their thoughts on children, they need to take time to discuss why they want or do not want children. Taking Planned Parenthood's Parenting Questionnaire (located on page 189 in the appendix) will give them a better idea whether they want to have children and if they are ready to start a family.

Upon completing their self-evaluations and exposing their thoughts about becoming parents, they may discover that they have changed their views and are no longer in agreement. If that's the case, they need to continue to discuss their differences, as a couple and in a calm manner, until they reach an amicable agreement that may include a compromise.

If Mary and Todd decide they want children, they need to pinpoint when. The couple should set a milestone or a date at which they will begin trying to conceive. Once that date is reached, if they are still wavering, then they need to uncover the hidden issue (or issues) that is blocking them from making progress. This is accomplished by willingly exploring the buried issues. Gridlock is usually experienced when one partner feels his or her lifelong dream is not being addressed or respected by the other. Personal dreams, wishes, goals, hopes, and aspirations in life are what give us purpose and a sense of meaning. Often identifying them will unveil the real issue at hand. A key element to saving and enriching your relationship or marriage is acknowledging and respecting each other's most precious personal hopes and wishes in life. Sometimes that includes the decision to have a baby.

When faced with a situation of him saying "Not Yet," you need to address the issue before it turns ugly:

+ Agree to talk about your conflict of "when."
+ Identify specifically what you want to accomplish.
+ Approach your conversations in a positive tone to keep the lines of communication open and increase your chances of reaching a resolution.
+ Take a break when you feel the conversation is becoming heated or you reach an impasse.
+ Share the responsibility equally for the resolution of your problem.
+ Communicate openly, listen actively, and acknowledge, accept, and respect each other's deepest dreams, wishes, hopes, and goals.

+ Be truthful about your wants.
+ Set an event or a timeline for when you will start trying to have a baby or when you will review where you are in the decision-making process.
+ If you find that your progress is blocked, uncover any hidden issues that are hindering your progress by looking at personal goals that you think are not being validated.

The importance of the manner in which you start your conversations cannot be stressed enough. If your talks begin in an angry tone, they will most likely have a negative ending. If you begin on a more positive note, you create a favorable atmosphere and will be more inclined to continue your conversations on that level. By doing so, you can significantly improve the effectiveness of your problem solving while developing a more positive perspective of each other and your relationship. Whether trying to solve differences about when to have children or another issue, couples that work together are more effective at problem solving than those that don't.

Relationships are filled with compromises and the decision to have, not to have, or to postpone children can hold a variety of solutions that each of you may find appealing. Whatever the solution, it must be specific enough to attract you to follow through without hesitation. A stronger, more satisfying relationship will evolve over time as each of you compromises equally.

Chapter 6

Additional Children

Many couples are happy with one child, but what if you want another child and your partner doesn't? How do you convince him that more children will be enjoyable, exciting, rewarding, and that you will have an even richer life? Or maybe you want another child, but you have financial or health concerns. Many women who think that it might be time to have another baby have questions like these and for good reason.

In the last two decades or so, family size has been changing. Women are having fewer children and waiting longer before starting a family. This table supplies some condensed statistics of women aged forty to forty-four (considered the end of the fertile period), courtesy of the U.S. Census Bureau.[1] The figures in the Average column indicate the average number of children born to women between the ages of forty and forty-four.

| Women Aged 40–44 by Number of Children They've Ever Born | | | | | |
Year	None	One	Two	Three +	Average
2002	17.9%	17.4%	35.4%	29.3%	1.930
1995	17.5%	17.6%	35.3%	29.9%	1.961
1990	16.0%	16.9%	35.0%	32.2%	2.045
1985	11.4%	12.6%	32.9%	43.1%	2.447
1980	10.1%	9.6%	24.6%	55.7%	2.998
1976	10.2%	9.6%	21.7%	58.6%	3.091

Two interesting points emerge from this census:

1. Over the past twenty-six years, the number of women having three or more children decreased 50 percent. This is a huge attitude shift for one generation. Women are clearly opting for smaller families, whether by choice, financial circumstance, or partnership stability (i.e., divorce). The average number of children birthed by women also dropped from three to slightly less than two.

2. The number of women with no children or one child has risen significantly. Women without children rose from 10.2 percent to 17.9 percent, while single-child women rose from 9.6 percent to 17.4 percent. More women are choosing not to have children or to have only one child.

What is not clear is the number of women who want more than one child and, for one reason or another, do not follow through. Most of the reasons a woman may want to expand her family could be very similar to the rationale for wanting a first baby:

+ She and her partner both really want a child.
+ She can afford to raise the child.
+ She fully expects that her health and the child's will be good.
+ She is prepared for any sacrifice to her career as a result of having a child and raising him or her.

There are, however, some unique feelings and questions that can enter into the decision of additional children. For example, is it better for my child to have a sibling, or should we stop at one? Is it okay for us to want to stop at one child? How long should we wait before getting pregnant again? In today's society, deciding to have additional children is a big decision that poses many questions for examination by both partners. Sometimes including the thoughts of current children can help, but this should never be the deciding factor. Dr. Kovacs and I do not like the idea of giving your existing children a voice in your decision to have another child. Children are just not mature enough to understand your needs and feelings. Giving them veto power, especially if they are older, sets a bad precedent in parent/child relations.

What Are Your Reasons?

Ask yourself why you think you may want more children and when you think would be the best time to have them. You and your partner may want to take a more objective look at your situation. You each should take a piece of paper and a pen and create a list of reasons that you want another child, as well as any doubts. Be honest when documenting your reasons, and after you have finished, be open when sharing your lists with each other. The same guidelines for discussion used in Chapter 3 may be applied here as well.

In most cases, since you already have one child, you know what to expect during labor and delivery, and while raising a baby and toddler. However, it is important that you agree that you are comfortable with all of the responsibilities involved in having more children.

Following are some additional reasons that could appear on your lists:

Strong Reasons to Have More Children
I want to pass on the love and camaraderie that I had growing up in my large family.

I was an only child. You may want a sibling for your child.

The experience of raising children truly fulfills me. Basically, your reasons for having this child may be the same reasons you had for your first one.

"Iffy" Reasons to Have Another Child

Time is running out for me. This is a reason that directly leads to the timing of when to have a child. How long can you wait? At what point does the delay add risk to a mother's health and the health of the baby? You and your partner need to engage in real, deep communication here. If your health or the new baby's health would be at risk, there are alternatives such as adoption or foster parenting that could be pursued in lieu of having another child.

My child wants and needs a playmate. If your child is lonely, you should address this immediately. Consider preschool or day-care facilities that stress interaction and learning. Trade off on babysitting with a neighbor or a relative's child, organize play activities at a nearby park with your neighbor's children, or explore other alternatives for younger children. If your child is older, enroll him or her in sports programs, Brownies, or Cub Scouts. Museums, the library, and clubs can provide interaction and stimulate your child's mind. If *you* want another baby, go for it. But if your child wants a sibling, and this is your reason for having another baby, find out what is missing in your child's life—in most cases a new baby will not fill that need anyway.

We have a son/daughter, now we want a daughter/son. Wanting a baby of the opposite gender from your first child is a perfectly natural feeling, however, this shouldn't be your only reason for wanting to expand your family. You need to understand your feelings and justification for wanting a baby of the opposite sex. Imagine that you go ahead, get pregnant, and have another baby of the same sex. Will this child be any less loved than your first? Will you continue to try again until you have a baby with the gender of your choice? If you want two children, then having one of each sex would be wonderful, but then so would having two girls or two boys.

I would like to have a child with my new husband. With second marriages becoming more common, this is a perfectly natural desire. Make sure that you have other reasons that will ensure that you both want and can handle the responsibilities of a child. We discuss second marriages and children in depth in Chapter 7.

We didn't do that good of a job raising our first child, and we want to do better with another one. Ask yourself exactly what you did wrong in raising your first child. Every parent makes mistakes and the firstborn tends to get the bulk of them. First children naturally tend to get more attention because they aren't competing with siblings. In most areas, this evens out. If you couldn't spend enough time with your firstborn, has your lifestyle changed to allow you to spend more time with your family? Is there any reason to believe that your lack of patience with your firstborn will improve when you have two children? You must determine if your belief represents the usual—and minor—regrets and mistakes that first-time parents will make, or if the experience is a result of some unresolved issues that you need to address prior to going forward with another child. If your experience was beyond the normal travails that first-time parents encounter, you need to understand why these mistakes occurred and how they can be corrected, perhaps, by taking a parenting class or seeing a therapist to discuss your concerns before having another child.

I was sedated during my first birth, and I want to experience child-birth in an alert state. This is also a perfectly natural desire, but because it belongs at number 999 of the "Iffy" reasons, you'd better have a list of reasons ahead of this one. Being conscious while giving birth to your child is one of nature's most magnificent experiences for many women. The birth of a child emphasizes that life is truly a miracle. However, if the major reason for having another child is that you want to be awake to experience the birth of your baby, you may want to examine your motives more closely. If you are alert during the birth, will you love your second child more than your first?

Unhealthy Reasons for Having Another Child

My family/friends are pressuring me to have another baby. Many relatives and friends will apply subtle, or not-so-subtle, pressure with comments such as, "When are you going to have another baby?" or, "Wouldn't Junior just love to have a little brother or sister?" and our favorite, "Oh, you <u>only</u> have one child?" This is *your* life and *your* family. Don't let someone else's bias on family size pressure you. Statistics clearly show that what may have been normal a generation ago has changed significantly today. Fewer and fewer women are opting to have additional children. If family and friends continue to pressure you, explain to them that you aren't ready, or that you don't want to have any more children, or just tell them that it's a personal matter that you would like to keep private.

My life is without meaning if I don't have another child. If this is one of the reasons on your list, we suggest that you take out another piece of paper and draft another list entitled "Things I Enjoy Doing." Odds are that you are not doing these things today, possibly because your current child takes time away from these activities. If you cannot fulfill your dreams with your first child, there is a high degree of probability that you will not be able to realize your personal goals by expanding your family. (That is unless your goal is to create your own hockey team or family band.) Bringing another child into your family with the sole purpose of giving your life meaning will not be healthy for you or for the child.

If we lose our first child, we'll still have another. Regardless of age, there is no guarantee of the amount of time we have on this earth. If you want to have another child because you fear losing your first, you may want to ask yourself why you fear losing your child? For example, did you or your partner experience the death of a sibling, a cousin, or a close friend as a child? Is there an inherited medical condition in your family that could be passed on to the next generation? Living with the fear of losing a child, without merit, needs to be addressed. You need to understand your fears about losing a child and how they are affecting you and your family. Respectfully, if you are in a situation in which your first child is terminally ill, this is a very painful and difficult time for all involved and you may want to seek out counseling. In times of crisis involving death or any other catastrophe or transition, most counselors suggest that you do not make any major life-altering decisions for a year, including having another child.

Having another baby will save my marriage. Having a baby will <u>not</u> save your marriage! Adding another child to an unstable marriage will most likely add anger, insecurities, self-doubt, and financial concerns to an already delicate situation. Do you seriously want to raise another child in this environment if you don't have to? Focus on saving your marriage first; then consider adding children.

We could use another tax deduction. Remember, this kid is going to cost you more than $161,000—that's far more than you'll receive in tax deductions.

My religion wants me to continue having more children. Some churches actively promote having children, the more the better, and discourage people from exercising choice about limiting the number of children they have through birth control. This pressure is very similar to pressures you may be getting from friends and relatives. If the problem escalates to the point where it affects you spiritually, talk to your church's leader and let him or her know what you are experiencing. If the problem persists, you will probably be more comfortable joining a church that is more respectful of your feelings.

Spacing Babies

Just when is the best time, physically and psychologically, to have another child? In a study published by the *New England Journal of Medicine* (Zhu, Rolfs, Nangle, and Horan, February 25, 1999), doctors found that waiting eighteen to twenty-three months after giving birth to your last child before conceiving another child was best for the new baby's health.[2] Babies conceived less that six months after a birth were 40 percent more likely to be born prematurely or underweight. The study attributes this to the mother's nutritional depletion and postpartum stress from the first birthing experience. The study also concluded that children conceived more than ten years after the mother's last birth faced double the risk of being born prematurely.

Psychologists commonly recommend spacing children at least three years apart.[3] In referring to these studies, Gayle Peterson, M.F.T., Ph.D., in an article on iVillage.com, says that the existing child thrives on undivided attention in his early years and that adding a sibling during these times could potentially give the existing child a sense of abandonment as attention shifts to the newborn. This can sometimes result in exaggerated rivalry and may influence his relationships as he grows older.

If you are considering another child, for both health and psychological reasons, spacing conception at least eighteen to twenty-three months apart seems to be ideal. Conceiving sooner introduces additional risks for both the newborn and the existing sibling. Lengthy time periods between births of eight to ten years can also add risks to the newborn and the mother since she is most likely an older mother. Any time you are considering having another child, you should first consult with your physician.

A Few Words about Only Children

You're still debating about having a second child and have concerns about what being an only child will mean to your firstborn. You may have heard only children can be bratty, loners, or, worse yet, little Poindexters! Fear not. Studies published by Dr. Toni Falbo of the University of Texas-Austin have found that only children are remarkably similar to firstborn children in multichild families.[4] Subtle differences between the two were that only children might not have as large a circle of friends as a child with siblings, but that both children have just as many close friends. Similarly, only children tend to join fewer afterschool activities than children with siblings, but they are more likely to be leaders in those organizations that they do join. Only children also tend to pursue their educations further than children with siblings, possibly as a result of fewer financial demands on the family. In brief, there appears to be very little statistical evidence that adding a second child will benefit your firstborn. So if you do want a second child, do so because you truly want another child and not for the welfare of your first child.

Brenda and Tom (first introduced on page 10) met through friends after college. Brenda quickly put Tom through her dating-criteria list of questions to determine if he would be second-date material. Brenda had come from a large close-knit family; there were family events throughout the year. She always wanted children and didn't want to take a chance on getting into a relationship with someone who felt otherwise. Tom came from a happy family, was particularly close with his brothers, and felt he wanted children at some point in his future. He passed her test and they were married three years later. Brenda's biggest attraction to her husband was the closeness that he had with his family.

They had openly talked about children during their dating period, and this continued after they married. During the first five years of marriage, Brenda and Tom focused on their careers, bought a house, traveled, went backpacking, hang-gliding, and camping, and had lots of fun with family and friends. After five years of fun, they decided it was time to have a baby.

Their first girl was colicky and had constant ear infections. They went through seven months of sleep deprivation taking turns attempting to calm their ailing child. When the doctor finally agreed to have tubes inserted into the baby's ears for relief, the young parents were near exhaustion. Their daughter improved, and one year later, Brenda wanted another baby. Tom was less than thrilled at the prospect.

Tom had concerns from their experience with their first daughter and was also worried about being able to handle the increasing responsibilities of a second child. He was anxious about finding time to get everything done—both the necessary household chores, plus fun things like family events and coaching a neighborhood T-ball team. They barely had time for all that now with just one child. Brenda convinced him that they would be able to handle the extra load and stressed how much better their daughter would be with a sibling. Her persuasion attempts worked. They had a second baby girl who slept through the night and had no colic problem or ear infections. After their second daughter was born, Tom said, "Absolutely no more children." Brenda understood and agreed.

About a year later, Brenda began having uncontrollable urges to have a third baby. She approached her husband. His response was definitive: "We're not having a third child!" Brenda persisted. For two years, she tried to talk with Tom twice a month about having another baby. Whenever she would bring up the subject, Tom would give the same automatic response.

Brenda was beside herself; she questioned why she had this obsessive desire to have another child when her husband didn't want any more. The overwhelming sensation to have another baby engulfed her and the emotion would not loosen its grip, no matter how much she tried to reason with herself. She talked with her family, their neighbors, and their friends—anyone who would listen.

Two years into their discussion about a third child, Brenda began to see a glimmer of hope in Tom's stance. She talked to her husband about how he was the third child in his family—the third boy. She asked Tom to think about how his parents would have felt if they hadn't had him. Brenda asked him to remember how happy his family was, the love they showered on him, and the joyful moments with his brothers. Tom pondered over his childhood and the fond memories he had and agreed with Brenda that he truly enjoyed being one of three children. At one point, he gave an ultimatum that if he agreed to have another child then they would get a swimming pool. Brenda was ecstatic and chased her husband into the bedroom.

Tom's decision to have a third child was touch-and-go though. Two weeks later he had changed his mind. Brenda was exhausted with the whole process and finally conceded defeat. She decided she would accept that she would have no more children and deal with her emotions and overcome her desires. Two weeks later, she discovered that she was pregnant with the "swimming pool" baby. Tom was not thrilled, but the next day he had the contractors in the backyard designing the new pool.

While Brenda was pregnant this time, two wives of Tom's best friends suffered miscarriages. His friends' losses made Tom realize what a miracle it was to be blessed with a healthy pregnancy. When his third daughter was born, Tom was elated and cried with joy in the delivery room.

Five months after the delivery, Brenda commented that the most rewarding memory about their decision-making process was "seeing my husband's happiness when our third daughter was born. He couldn't stop crying—there was complete and total love for her. Also, what's most rewarding is hearing Tom say to family and friends how blessed we are to have three beautiful healthy girls. It's very comforting. He's done a complete 180 degree turn-around."

What Worked:

+ When Brenda changed her mind and knew she wanted a third child, she was open to discussing her feelings with Tom.
+ Brenda kept the communication going even when it wasn't appreciated and made sure that Tom knew her mindset.
+ When Brenda began to get that strong desire again after the second baby, she questioned why the urges kept recurring. Since Brenda came from a large family, she recognized that part of her yearning was related to the good experiences she'd had in her childhood. Consciously or not, she was able to get Tom to also look into his childhood and recall his own positive experiences of being a third child.
+ Tom's compromise of a pool for a baby was an unintended good idea. With a pool, Tom and Brenda can arrange to have family and friends meet at their house for get-togethers. This is easier on them with three children and accomplishes Tom's goal of staying close to family and friends.
+ When two of Tom's friends lost their babies during Brenda's third pregnancy, Tom did not translate those miscarriages into possible

problems for their baby. He was thankful that their pregnancy was going well.

What Didn't Work:

+ Brenda began pressuring Tom for a second child when they were still too emotionally frazzled from their current baby's difficult first year. Letting Tom know her desire was okay, but adding the pressure of constant discussions when they were tired led to Tom's stonewalling.

+ Given the health issues of the first child, conceiving another child so soon after giving birth would have added increased risk to the second birth.

+ Tom and Brenda never discussed and agreed upon how many children they wanted. They also never discussed spacing of the babies. Brenda appeared to always want another baby within one year of giving birth.

+ Immediately after their second birth, Brenda quickly agreed to Tom's demand that they have no more children. The easiest time to get a woman to agree to no more children is right after a birth. We wouldn't expect Tom to know this, but a woman would—especially one who has experienced the pain of childbirth.

+ Their third baby was decided by an "oops." Everything worked out well in this case, but oops is never a good reason for deciding to have a child.

Analysis

The decision-making process for Tom and Brenda was a test of endurance, control, and compromise. Brenda continued to persevere through talks with Tom about her wish to have another child. She also questioned the depth of her desire and her own reasoning for another baby. Tom continued to control the decision by stalemating and then, in a moment of weakness, agreed to another child with the compromise of getting a swimming pool. He overcame his fear of having a third child when he witnessed his close friends' loss of their babies through miscarriage. This made him realize what a miracle it was to be able to create a human being and how blessed he and his wife were. In the delivery room Tom welcomed his new daughter with tears of joy, indicating that he had more than enough love to share for all three girls. Although it was difficult, Brenda and Tom kept open communication throughout their decision-making process. They knew how to talk, listen, and compromise, and they knew how to make decisions together. As a result, they will most likely remain in a successful marriage.

Another couple, Roberta and Carlos, had some difficulty with the decision to have their first and second children. Carlos was fearful that bringing a child into the marriage would create divorce and cause pain to all parties involved—an experience he'd had with his own parents. Together, they discussed his childhood issues; he sought counseling, resolved many of his fears, and agreed to have a baby.

Their first son was such a pleasure that about two years later Roberta wanted to have another as a companion or play buddy for him. But Carlos was completely opposed to having more children—this time for a different reason.

Carlos's eighteen-year-old nephew had recently been involved in an accident and had died. Carlos was close to his nephew and was deeply saddened by his death. Carlos became fearful of the pain associated with losing a loved one. While he mourned his nephew's death, he also watched his sister grieve. Carlos knew he would be devastated if anything happened to their current son and didn't want to add to this by bringing another child into the world, one who might die and add to his grief.

Carlos went back to counseling to deal with the loss of his nephew and his fears of losing his son. Once Carlos resolved his issues associated with the death of his nephew, he and Roberta were able to talk constructively about expanding their family and how that would change their current lives. They talked for a couple of months until they finally agreed they were both ready to add another person to their family.

Today, Roberta and Carlos have six-month-old and four-year-old boys. Carlos periodically tells Roberta that they are so blessed to have two beautiful healthy boys. He's even approached Roberta about having a third.

What Worked:

+ Both Roberta and Carlos recognized that he had some personal psychological issues to resolve prior to agreeing to become a parent.
+ Carlos sought professional help and resolved his fears.
+ When Carlos began to have reservations about having a second child, due to his fear that the child might die, he quickly sought help again. Carlos recognized that his fears would not go away on their own and would need to be resolved therapeutically.

Analysis

Roberta and Carlos approached each decision to have a child realistically and intelligently. They expressed their desires, discussed their views thoroughly, and then resolved any issues together and with the assistance of a therapist. They made sure that they were ready to have a child and that they would not have to face any of their personal baggage. This is the ideal way to approach the decision to have a child.

Cathy and Ernie were high school sweethearts and married right after graduation. They both wanted children but couldn't decide on how many. Cathy always dreamed about having six children while Ernie only wanted two. They had a daughter one year after they married and four years later, a son. Ernie was happy. He had the two children of his dreams, life was perfect with Cathy, and he didn't want any more kids. Getting a vasectomy was frightening to him and he didn't like Cathy's mood swings from taking birth control pills, so he asked her to get a tubal ligation.

Cathy still wanted more children and tried to talk with Ernie about it, but he stood his ground. Their one-sided, heated discussions went on for about a year when Cathy finally acquiesced and agreed not to have any more children. With pressure from Ernie and much reluctance, Cathy scheduled an appointment to get a tubal ligation to prevent further pregnancies. Since she was committed to the marriage, she underwent the surgical procedure for him, convincing herself that she didn't want to have any more children with her husband.

A year after she got her tubes tied, Cathy and Ernie divorced. He ended up marrying another woman who wanted children and he accommodated her wishes. Cathy later met and married a wonderful man who accepted her two children and wanted more. Unfortunately, Cathy's tubal ligation was not reversible and her dream of having a large family was shattered.

What Worked:
+ For Cathy and Ernie, their decisions to have two children worked very well.
+ What also worked is that they are now both in happy and stable relationships . . . with other people.

What Didn't Work:
+ Cathy and Ernie were very young to be making some of the life decisions that they made. Marrying at eighteen and having a child at nineteen is an awful lot of pressure to place on people who are still maturing emotionally. Having discussions about vasectomies and tubal ligations in their mid- to late twenties, when they still had almost twenty years of baby potential together, was disastrous.
+ Ernie and Cathy had some inadequate birth control advice. There are options other than the pill and vasectomies that are safe and reliable.
+ All discussions were one-sided and heated—in other words, completely unproductive. Ernie drew a line in the sand and wouldn't even discuss the issue with Cathy. Cathy should have seen this as a clear indicator that there was something going on with Ernie that evoked anger and defiance whenever they discussed having

more children. Ernie was showing either emotional immaturity or some deep-seated problem that was seriously affecting their marriage. The fact that Cathy couldn't see this and went ahead with the tubal ligation was unfortunate.

+ Cathy underwent a tubal ligation even though she didn't want the operation. In her late twenties, she made a life-altering decision that she didn't have to make.

Analysis

Given their ages, this couple should have focused their energies from a hard "no way" into a softer "not yet." Recognizing that they were not ready as a couple to have children would have allowed them to mature emotionally, establish themselves financially, and revisit the idea of having children in the future.

Deciding to have additional children is a huge choice that needs mutual support and commitment. You want to ensure that you and your partner are on the same page about having another child. Take a look at why you want to have more children. Are your reasons solid or are they iffy and even unreasonable? The best reasons for wanting additional children are that you and your partner want another child, you are financially capable of supporting an additional child, you have every reason to believe that both you and the child will be healthy, and you are willing to sacrifice any career interruptions that may occur as a result. If you have differences, follow the ground rules from Chapter 3 to help guide you to a successful outcome. And, if you find that you have come to a stalemate, recognize that you may need professional assistance through the help of a licensed family counselor.

Chapter 7

Second Marriages

I f you are in a second marriage, or about to enter into a second marriage, and you are contemplating having children, you are not alone. The majority of people who divorce will remarry. Interestingly, the median age of women who remarry is thirty-two years old—well within peak childbearing years.[1] For men, the remarrying age is thirty-four years old—also well within the time when they would most likely want children. Most second marriages are faced with unique challenges in the first few months and even years ahead, but take solace in the fact that millions of women share similar challenges.

Complexities of Second Marriages

Second marriages offer fresh hope of gaining happiness not achieved in the first union. The bad news is that they frequently come with additional complications, popularly called "baggage." Any unresolved issues from a previous marriage need to be seriously addressed to minimize the impact on the new union. Often, those issues will include children from a previous marriage, or the decision to have children with a new spouse. Many couples who have not sought therapy or have not resolved their feelings do not learn from the first marriage and they end up repeating the same issues in the second marriage.

With second marriages having a 60 percent divorce rate, you may want to first ensure you are selecting the "right" partner for you.[2] If you want to continue the relationship and have any reservations, talk to a licensed therapist or clergy member for assistance in evaluating your compatibility. Many licensed therapists or clergy members have been certified to provide couples with a highly reliable Prepare-MC questionnaire. Dr. Kovacs uses this tool quite often to measure how couples agree/disagree on a number of items, such as expectations, communication, conflict, sex, money, children, friends, family, and a few more items. These questions are valid for identifying areas of discord, and they give the couple a more realistic view of marriage.

If there are children from a previous marriage, don't rush into trying to have another child. Your children will need time to adjust to their new situation and living arrangements. They are still recovering from the major upheaval of the breakup of their family of origin, as well as adjusting to part-time parents and moving out of their home. Just as your children need time to settle into their new circumstances, so do you! Spend extra time with your children (especially your biological children, but also your stepchildren). You'll likely find that in helping them accept your new situation, they're also helping you cope.

The faster you rush the process of a new baby, the higher your risks of family discontent. Your stepchildren will not share in the bliss of your new relationship, and acceptance may take time—in some cases, years. This is especially true if the stepchild only visits on weekends and holidays. Children from a previous marriage will need time to learn how to relate to a new adult in the family, and the stepparent will need time to become acquainted and then to develop a relationship with the children. Counseling at this important stage in your children's development can help the family understand their issues and help you as a parent learn how to address them. School counselors and marriage and family therapists are excellent sources for help. There also are resources available from the Stepfamily Foundation, *www.stepfamily.org*, and there may be a group for stepparents in your city that will be very supportive of a blended family. Patience, time, and understanding are necessary for the development of familial relationships, and implementation of a plan of assurance to provide stability to the children is critical to the success of this transition.

No Previous Children Involved

At least one of you is divorced or widowed. If there were no children from the first marriage, how was the decision made not to have children in the first marriage? If one of you is divorced, and having children was a factor in the decision to divorce (yours or his), make sure that you both understand how this occurred, and what has changed since that marriage. A deeper question is why did the marriage dissolve? What needs were not being fulfilled? If you are both confident that there were no "children" issues in the first marriage(s), then you can begin asking yourselves the same questions as if this were your first relationship.

He Has a Child(ren) from His Previous Marriage

In all likelihood, you will be the weekend or summer stepmother to his children while his ex-wife will likely have custody of the child during the week. Is your husband emotionally ready to begin another family? If he feels as though he failed as a father the first time, he needs to discuss those feelings so you both will understand his reservations. If he's dragging his feet about if and when you will have children together, you need to find out what his concerns are. His reluctance and fears are understandable, given his first experience with marriage and parenthood.

How do his children get along with him? If there are difficulties, you will need to be patient and supportive while he deals with the children, who are hurt and angry about the divorce. It's important to find out as much as possible about what led to divorce in his first marriage before you marry him. You must also understand that you are only getting one side of the story. Uncovering the issues has to be done with a great deal of tact and empathy. Remember, the wounds of divorce can take from three to five years to heal. Try to find out how the relationship was prior to the separation and divorce. If there are or were issues, what steps have been taken to avoid a repetition in his future relationships?

If his children are involved in afterschool activities, your husband (or husband-to-be) should be a willing participant. If he is not, find out why. Your role in afterschool activities may be an issue, but his role definitely should not be.

How old are his children? If his children are already grown, he's likely to be in his forties or fifties and may not share your enthusiasm for having toddlers again. He's at the age when most men are becoming grandparents, and many men (and women) are experiencing a midlife itch (which may have contributed to the divorce). If you are fertile, find out what his thoughts and feelings are about having another child or children as soon as you can, in the early stages of the relationship—especially if you still want children. For many middle-aged men, having a child can reinvigorate their lives. There are many men who say having a baby was the best thing that ever happened to them. However, if he is focused on retirement planning, shuffleboard, or sailing to Tahiti, he's not likely to be excited about the pitter-patter of little feet interrupting his naps (unless the grandkids are over) on a Saturday afternoon.

How will the alimony/child support payments affect your financial ability to have and raise your first child? You knew going into the marriage that he had outside financial responsibilities. In addition to monthly child support, there may also be health insurance costs and the funding of the child's college education. If you are contemplating marriage to a man who has these financial obligations, you must consider how this will impact your relationship and adjust accordingly. Remember, he is taking his parental responsibilities seriously, and that deserves your respect.

If he's a "Deadbeat Dad," expect that very likely he will repeat this behavior with you and your child later.

You Have a Child(ren) from a Previous Marriage

Most likely, your child is living with you and your new husband. How well does your husband handle being a stepdad? If he's tentative, make sure you both know why and help him overcome his unease if possible. Apprehensive behavior is common among stepparents. Discipline issues and heart-to-heart discussions usually occur only with the child and his biological parent. Disciplining of your child should be discussed before marriage or very early in the relationship, especially if the biological father is involved in the care of the child on a regular basis. The stepfather would do well to concentrate on becoming friends first before trying.

If you decide to have a child together, is your husband willing to share his attention with his stepson once your new baby is born? Newborns commonly receive extra attention, but this will also be a critical time for you to share with your other children. During this time, it is imperative that your husband helps out with your first child's needs. This will strengthen the bond between the two and assure the child that she is an integral part of the family. Make sure your husband is up for this.

If the divorce was difficult and you are still angry, can you and your new husband remain calm in front of your child (or stepchild)? The child has already been through enough pain, confusion, and possibly even self-blame. Your child should never hear or see any anger toward ex-spouses. This is especially true for your current husband, who will obviously want to protect you and may display anger in doing so. Your ability to control emotions over frustrating ex-spousal issues will be an indicator of how well the two of you will handle any future issues between your new child and the stepchild, and any absent relatives.

You Both Have Children from Previous Marriages

Assuming that you have been together for at least several months, you are starting to get used to being a blended family. You already have some experience with how his kids relate to your kids, how well it's going with the ex-spouses, and how well each of you are managing a complex family. What are the problems occurring in the new family? If the children are not getting along, you need to understand and address the conflicts. Bringing another child into the family dynamic now is not going to improve family harmony. Ideally, when you are ready to add a new child, the existing children have accepted the divorce (although some never do), reconciled any ill will toward their new stepparent, and are ready to continue their growing up, albeit in a situation that they may not completely accept. Don't expect the stepchild, or your child, to love her new situation or to love her new stepparent. Do expect her to respect your positions as heads of the family. Depending on the circumstances, there may always be issues with the stepchildren regarding the breakup of the original family. This is normal, but they need to feel included and to be open to the expansion of their new family. Their buy-in to having a new baby will give them greater acceptance of the baby and your marriage, and greater confidence that they are part of the family.

If either you, your husband, or both of you are still having difficulties adjusting to the family situation as it is currently, this may not be the right time to add the complexities that a newborn will bring. Your new baby should not have to deal with your old baggage (babies come with their own baggage—diapers, bottles, and blankets!). There will be integration issues, as there are with any child with siblings, but try to resolve as much of your old baggage as possible. Not only does your new baby deserve this, so do you!

How to Prepare the Family When You Want a Baby

Your existing children (biological and step) will need to be prepared for the family addition. As we said earlier, try to resolve the issues incurred in the making of the blended family by spending time with the children. If there is more than one child, make sure that each child has "special time" with his biological parent to sustain that relationship. "Family time" is also important, as it will bring everyone closer. It is very important that you don't try to force your stepchildren's affections. Those feelings will build gradually as the children accept their situation and grow to know their stepparent.

This is also the time to address issues with counselors. Your goal is for the existing children to face only the normal issues that children face when they get a baby brother or sister. You're probably not going to achieve this (don't sweat it if you don't) because blended families will always have issues like visitation and child support payments. But if you work toward harmony and acceptance, you can minimize much of the insecurities of the existing children and many of the frustrations for the parents.

Be honest with your children when you become pregnant. Let them share your experiences as your tummy grows. Again, they may not totally embrace the situation, but they need to learn to accept it and respect what is happening. Once the baby is born, make sure that they still have their "private time," especially with their biological parent. If you're the biological parent, the time burden can seem overwhelming, but your husband can do a lot to help give you the time necessary for your other children.

Kids are smart enough to realize that their baby brother or sister has needs, but they can easily (and wrongly) conclude that they are no longer as important to you now that you and your spouse have your own baby. If your child is old enough, let him help you with the baby. Don't give him only the dirty work (kids quickly realize what's going on and will resent it); give him some meaningful responsibilities. Above all, find the time to spend with each of the kids, privately and together. With the responsibilities of a newborn, this will be difficult, but do it! Your husband's cooperation and participation at this time is essential.

If more than one stepchild is involved, you may find that the eldest stepchild experiences the hardest adjustment. This usually results from this child having the most awareness of what went on during the divorce. The eldest child is often the most sensitive to her place when families merge. She may feel threatened that the bond she had with her biological parent is now threatened with a newborn. In this situation, the biological parent needs to set aside additional time with the child to reassure her that their relationship is solid. The stepparent should also be involved, but not at the expense of the parent. If problems persist, address them quickly through family counseling.

The grandparents and other family members (including the ex-spouses) can also play a vital role in making sure that the children adjust well to their new situations. There will be times when both families are together in support of the child's activities (graduations, birthdays, sports, etc.). If all parties in attendance can accept one another by being polite and acknowledging the nonrelated children, a lot of questions and hurt feelings will be avoided.

Prepare your relatives and friends for your decision to have a baby by telling them that you've decided to have another child (details are not necessary) and express your hope that they can accept your decision. When you tell your ex and his family, impress upon them your desire for acceptance of the new child and for a stable relationship for all. If they have any questions or issues, try to resolve them. Once the emotions of the divorce have subsided, most people will do what they can for the children's benefit. If issues cannot be resolved to your and your husband's satisfaction, you may want to limit ex-spouses' access to the children (as a group). The age of your existing children will also affect their awareness of what is happening within the families and with their friends. An older child will better understand that the divorce is why Uncle Charlie doesn't come around anymore, whereas a three-year-old will be confused.

Bottom line, remember that your jobs as parents are to make sure that each child feels safe and secure, is loved, and receives guidance as he or she progresses through the beginning of life. Yes, problems will occur more with blended families than traditional families. What you both need to do is accept that "stuff" will happen, make sure that you are capable and willing to address the "stuff," and that you have a plan in place on how to deal with the "stuff" when and if it occurs. Be optimistic about the birth of your new baby, but be realistic by being ready for problems.

Following are a few examples of second marriages, blended families, and how the couples resolved their differences on having another child.

Scott had full custody of his four children from his first marriage, when he married Carolyn. Although Carolyn was fifteen years younger than Scott and had no kids, Scott communicated to her, shortly before the marriage, that he really didn't want any more children. Carolyn accepted his children, ranging from ages eight to sixteen, and they, in turn, liked her. Carolyn never actually verbally agreed not to have a child and about a year into the marriage became persistent with her need to have a baby. For Scott, life was much easier with Carolyn in his life, She had become a mother to his four children; they had all accepted her. Scott finally agreed to have one child with her. Carolyn gave birth to a little girl and everyone in the family doted on the new addition, including Scott.

Carolyn decided she wanted a second child. Scott flatly refused. They got pregnant by having unprotected sex unbeknownst to Scott and delivered a healthy baby boy. Scott resented his new son and treated him like an unwanted child. As a result, their youngest son turned out to be the "bad" kid in the family. Scott distanced himself from Carolyn and even committed adultery.

Scott and Carolyn now have been married for more than twenty years, but it has not been a solid union. A lot of counseling got them through their difficult times. Scott and his youngest son are now close, and they have worked through the issues of Scott's not wanting his son around when he was younger.

What Worked:
+ Scott's first agreement to have a child with Carolyn was consensual.
+ The family accepted the first daughter with open arms.
+ Carolyn and Scott eventually sought counseling, and Scott finally accepts his youngest child.

What Didn't Work:

+ Carolyn and Scott did not have a firm agreement on additional children when they married.
+ Carolyn had a second child without Scott's agreement.
+ Scott did not accept the second child and treated him poorly.
+ Scott and Carolyn did not address issues until problems festered and Scott committed adultery.

Analysis

Unfortunately, this is a classic example of the impact that not agreeing can have on a relationship. Carolyn and Scott had an initial agreement (reluctantly from Scott) about their first child together, and it went well. However, their second child together was Carolyn's decision alone, which resulted in Scott's long-standing, simmering resentment. His behavior was his way of punishing both his wife and his son for her betrayal. Counseling got them through their difficult times, including the reconciliation between Scott and his youngest son. In Dr. Kovacs's experience, children and their parents usually have a difficult time with reconciliation until the child has reached adulthood.

When You Already Have Children and Want More . . . with Him

Sarah and Jack both had custody of their children from previous marriages (see page 12). Jack's two girls and Sarah's three boys ranged in age from three to eight. During their courtship, they did a lot of kid activities, including soccer, T-ball, and birthday celebrations. Jack and Sarah's relationship blossomed, their kids seemed to get along well, and so they decided to marry. Over the next two years, they experienced some blended family issues, but because of their patience and understanding they adjusted well to their new lives. The children were raised with equal discipline and love—Jack accepted Sarah's boys and Sarah accepted Jack's girls.

After a few years of their marriage, Sarah decided she wanted another baby. When she approached Jack about this, he was surprised. They had been married only two years, and he was just getting used to all the stress and added expense of five children. Adding another child would mean more responsibility, more expense, more refereeing, more chaos, and one more child to worry about. Jack was happy with the situation with five children, but he wasn't interested in expanding his family to six kids and relayed this to Sarah.

Sarah's position was that another child would solidify their marriage and more strongly unite their two families into one. She felt this was true deep in her heart and communicated this to Jack. Again, Jack said no. Tension arose immediately between them on this subject. Each time Sarah tried to approach the subject, Jack didn't want to talk, creating a distance that hadn't existed before.

Raising five young children, each needing individual attention, did not leave much private time for Jack and Sarah. Jack relished this time and didn't want to spend it talking about whether to have more children. Still, Sarah tried to tell him why it was so important for her to have another child: She explained they were financially stable, she was a stay-at-home mom, and she would take on most of the responsibilities of raising another baby. Jack said, "I'm having a hard enough time keeping track of all our kids' names. Another kid would be one more name I'd have to run through my list before getting it right. Six kids is a hockey team!" Sarah laughed at first, but then she realized Jack was serious.

They continued to hold firm for six months. Then Sarah, even though she was on the pill, realized that she was two months late with her period. She took a home pregnancy test and discovered that she was pregnant. When she told Jack, he was upset but supported her pregnancy.

Throughout Sarah's pregnancy, all the children were excited about a new baby in their house. Jack even seemed excited. He was there in the delivery room; he cut the umbilical cord and wept when he held his son Tyler for the first time. When Jack and Sarah brought Tyler home, their children accepted him with open arms.

Today, there is always some type of activity going on in Sarah and Jack's household. They have not formed a hockey team yet. Thankfully, the older children are always helping out with the younger ones, and they all feel responsible for looking after Tyler. Jack says that he is amazed at how much he enjoys his entire family and how Tyler seems to have pulled them all together tighter than before. Sarah is overjoyed.

What Worked:
+ Sarah and Jack's family was blended when discussions began.
+ There was open communication between the couple.
+ Sarah did not overrule Jack's choice—oops does happen.
+ The children helped out with the new baby.

What Didn't Work:
+ Sarah and Jack did not agree on an additional child.
+ They didn't discuss their positions and didn't find out each other's dreams or visions for their future.

Analysis

The strong family unit helped make a potentially bad situation okay. Jack was mature enough to know that accidents happen—the pill is not 100 percent effective. Once they faced the cards that were dealt, everyone adjusted and moved on.

If you are in a second marriage or contemplating a second marriage, wanting to have "one of ours" is a natural feeling, but you need to keep things in perspective. Don't rush into having a child especially if other kids are involved. Get family issues on track (you don't have to be issue-free, just have them under control). Make sure having kids was not an issue in your or his previous marriage. Ensure that you and your partner are spending quality time with your biological children and stepchildren, and with each other. Make sure finances are okay to support a new baby. Respect your husband's concerns if he is older. If you have opposing views, acknowledge the differences that need to be addressed in your marriage and take advantage of your additional experience to handle problem areas by recognizing them quickly and dealing with them maturely.

Blended families can be challenging and adding another child to the equation can be a delicate matter. During this period of transition, the key to success is patience, time, and understanding for the entire family as a whole.

Chapter 8

The V Word—Vasectomies

With the divorce rate hovering near 50 percent, it is inevitable that following a divorce, many men will choose to remarry. In many instances, these men will already have had children and will choose to get a vasectomy. Many women will then find themselves in a situation where they have fallen in love with a divorced man who has already had children and can't have more without a surgical procedure.

Each year, roughly half a million men request vasectomies as a form of birth control and approximately 5 percent (one out of twenty) change their minds some time after the procedure.[1] The success rate for the reversal is over 95 percent.

For those of you not familiar with vasectomies, here's what a man goes through. His first step is to make an appointment with a urologist who explains the procedure and informs him it is a permanent alteration and that some pain will be involved. He is also told that after the surgery, he will need to be careful about lifting heavy objects for four to six weeks.

The urologist may recommend that the patient take some time to reflect on the impact and the implications that this procedure will have on his life, particularly if he intends to marry again. After the consultation, most men give serious thought and consideration to their decision to have a vasectomy and how this will affect their future relationships. This decision should not be made with the same quick enthusiasm of a Tijuana tattoo on a drunken Saturday night. Usually a significant period, sometimes weeks or months, is taken to make the decision.

Most men choose to have a vasectomy with no possibility, in their minds, of reversal. Sometimes though, circumstances may arise in close relationships that will create doubt. The most common reason for men to consider a reverse vasectomy (vasovasostomy in medical terminology) is a remarriage and the desire to start all over again.[2] He may have lost his wife and/or a child; or he may have married again and his next wife is insistent on having a child with him.

If you want children and the man of your dreams has had a vasectomy, be prepared for some long discussions. Remember, only one out of twenty men who have had a vasectomy are willing to have the procedure reversed.[3]

If one of your goals in marrying is to have a baby, you will need to be very honest with him and very respectful of why he underwent the vasectomy in the first place. You must understand that he underwent a serious medical procedure in an area that is very near and dear to him. The time he took, from making the first appointment to setting the date of the surgery, was to resolve any doubts about fathering additional children. Having empathy for what he experienced will help you move forward in your endeavor to persuade him to change his mind.

To get him to *want* a reversal, he needs to be convinced that his mindset has changed since the procedure. You will have to demonstrate to him specifically how your future will be improved with the reversal. You will have to convince him of your support and willingness to stay with him throughout the procedure and the pain. Both of you will take responsibility for the costs associated with the reversal and both of you will share the benefits and the rewards together. See page 102 of this chapter to learn more about the vasovasostomy process, but bear in mind that the cost will be at least $5,000–$10,000, which is usually not covered by medical insurance.

For second marriages, when one spouse wants a baby, a vasectomy can be an enormous issue, as it was for Bill and Gail. Bill was married once before, at a young age. He and his first wife had a son together and divorced four years later. At the time, he thought he didn't want any more children, and underwent a vasectomy. Then about eight years later, Bill met Gail. She knew about his vasectomy from the beginning and seemed to accept it, so the relationship blossomed. After a couple of years of being together, they were married. Gail was thirty-one and Bill was thirty-nine. At that time wanting children was not an issue for either of them.

As Gail got older she began to feel the need to have children, while Bill continued to remain firm about not wanting another child. The issue to have children developed into a bone of contention.

They talked on and off for a tense year with Gail initiating each conversation about wanting to start a family and Bill getting a reverse vasectomy. Together, they reviewed their circumstances: Financially, they were prepared to have children. Gail did not need to work if they had a child. They owned their home, and they agreed that Bill could continue enjoying his freedom to travel when he felt the urge. By building on these agreements, Gail eventually convinced Bill that he had the patience to make a good father and that any changes to their relationship would be a net positive to him.

Fifteen years after Bill got a vasectomy, he underwent the procedure to reverse it. Bill had to have the operation twice because he developed keloid scarring (hard scars around the area where the stitches were). The scarring from the first attempted reversal sealed everything off, so Bill's doctor had to go in and remove the scar tissue in a second operation. Gail told us later that Bill was so upset about the operations—especially the second—that at one point he told her angrily he'd never wanted to have the reversal done in the first place. However, after the operation was over and Bill had healed, the tension between the couple vanished. They now have two beautiful boys, and another child on the way.

Bill said about his newfound fatherhood, "I wouldn't change anything for the world. It's been a fantastic experience. I think when you become a parent you automatically develop a greater sense of patience for children, especially your own. In all actuality, I really didn't like being around kids prior to having my own. It's sad to say, but looking back on it now, I didn't ever have a relationship with my son from my first marriage until after he became a teenager. We have a great relationship today, but not when he was a child and needed me the most. I wasn't ready for parenthood back then. And, because of my past reactions to children in general and my past experience at being a father, I honestly thought I wouldn't make a good father the second time around. Gail convinced me otherwise. And I'm glad she did because I'm a much better father today than I ever was before. Perhaps it's because I'm older and have a greater appreciation for children, at least for our own. There's something that happens when you're ready to be a parent. Look at me now. I'm really enjoying it this time. Just ask my wife. I can't wait to get home to be with my sons."

What Worked:

+ Gail's initial acceptance of Bill's vasectomy when they first met worked well for the couple. It wasn't a turnoff for her at the time because she did not have strong feelings about having children. Bill felt he could have the life he envisioned with Gail without the complications of children.

+ When Gail started to change her mind, she openly communicated her wants and her reasons as she understood them, and she was persistent in maintaining dialogue and empathy for Bill's position; he realized how important children were for her.

+ Bill may not have always wanted the discussions, but the conversations did take place in an atmosphere of acceptance and understanding. The couple stopped when their conversations turned argumentative.

- Throughout the process, Gail never pushed Bill to curtail his travel desires, or any of his personal activities. Over time, Bill changed these on his own as other things became more important to him.
- The couple reviewed important facts that needed to be considered when deciding whether to have children.
- This process reinvigorated Bill's relationship with his first child, bringing his son back into his life.

What Didn't Work:
- Gail's change of mind about not wanting children did not go over well for Bill. He was afraid that his lifestyle would be negatively affected if he relented. Until Bill was convinced otherwise, he dug in his heels, resisting any change.
- Bill perceived Gail as being coercive and he felt he had to resist her efforts to get a reverse vasectomy. As long as he felt that any decision he made was to appease his wife, he could not make an independent decision of his own accord.
- The procedure did not work the first time. The added surgery gave Bill an additional reason to regret his decision to give in to Gail's request for a reversal.

Analysis

This was a highly difficult time for Gail and Bill's marriage. Gail was aware of Bill's vasectomy from the beginning and although she agreed before marriage to live child-free, she changed her mind when her maternal instincts took over. Initially, this left Bill feeling as though he had been betrayed. Fortunately, Gail was able to communicate her new wants, desires, and dreams for their future together; in turn, Bill was able to express his own thoughts and feelings honestly and openly to Gail. Although Gail was persistent to the point that Bill felt pressured to get a vasovasostomy to save the marriage, he was able to assert himself and tell her how pressured he felt, and she was able to realize the effect her persistence was having on him.

Gail took a risk pushing Bill to the point of having to choose between his marriage to her and the vasovasostomy. Bill felt he was in a no-win situation. If he refused to have the reversal done, it could have meant the end of the marriage. If he had the reversal done only to pacify his wife and save the marriage, he would have felt deeply resentful. The fact that Gail and Bill had reached this position indicated that their communication had broken down during their discussions. This would have been a perfect place to bring in a qualified therapist to help them get through their gridlock.

As a result of both taking a stand and being willing to hear each other, they were able to change their approaches to listening more attentively, validating each other's objections, and making a strong effort to understand each other. With time and care, both partners began to perceive the importance of their sharing and reached a mutual agreement.

Fortunately, the operation was an eventual success. Bill adjusted beautifully to being a parent, and even resuscitated his relationship with his first child.

When a relationship reaches this critical point, each partner needs to step back to understand what the issues are, what is at stake, and what the consequences are of any decision or indecision. A therapist can assist a couple by pointing out where they are in the decision-making process and helping them through their emotions. Bill could have explored more thoroughly why he originally got the vasectomy and compared that point in his life to where he was with Gail. Gail could have better understood where she was pushing the relationship and if she really meant to pose her desire to have children as a marriage ultimatum. Gail and Bill have made the right choice because they are still happy as a couple and are ecstatic about being parents.

The situation Gail and Bill found themselves in was probably more typical than what my husband and I experienced. Ken and I fell in love and got married with my believing that he would have his vasectomy reversed (and Ken's having no recollection of this agreement). After our wedding, when my biological clock was on full tilt, Ken would not commit to the operation. My fortieth birthday marked the beginning of our many long discussions about children, his fears, and our goals in life. We openly talked about every two weeks over an eight-month period trying to resolve our differences on children. We agreed to listen to each other with empathy, to take breaks when things got too heated, and to continue to work on our problem until we had an amicable agreement.

We discussed why we felt the way we did about children, why it was so important for us to have or not have children. To help Ken get a sense of parenthood, I arranged for my niece and nephew to spend a weekend to expose Ken to the joys of having children around—the results were less than satisfying (see Chapter 4, page 47). While my intentions were good, the experience only convinced Ken that he was right not to want children because he did not like taking care of other people's kids. Then, through a friend, I even found another couple that had undergone the reversal and arranged for us to spend an afternoon together.

Throughout our ordeal, while I advocated the joys of children to support the decision I wanted, Ken continued stonewalling. My perception was that Ken was stalling the decision until such time as I would no longer be able to conceive or I would give up. On the positive side, Ken talked to another man who had gone through a vasovasostomy; that helped reduce Ken's fears about the operation.

Ken told me that the best thing about the whole decision-making process was that he really enjoyed talking with me. Even though we had not yet resolved our differences, we were learning more about each other, which was making our relationship more enjoyable.

Ken finally decided to get his vasectomy reversed. When I asked him what changed his mind, he said, "What really changed my mind to get my vasectomy reversed was realizing the strength of our relationship and wanting to keep it strong. It was also difficult for me to see the woman I love go through emotional turbulence. With this, I realized that it was okay for me to be open to the possibility of children in our lives. I had been on a ninety-degree pendulum against having children and now I was thinking that the pendulum had swung more toward the middle. I wasn't completely convinced that I would be a good father, but this philosophy was good enough for me to go through with a vasovasostomy. A small amount of my decision was due to curiosity. But, I did this mainly for my wife and partly for us."

I was fully convinced that Ken really wanted children when we met with the urologist. Ken told the doctor that the reason he wanted to get a vasovasostomy was because he wanted to try to have children. Ken admitted that he was a little nervous about the operation, but added that he was more interested in becoming a father. I was elated to hear this. Ken underwent the vasovasostomy successfully and was pronounced fertile during a follow-up visit with his doctor. Three months later, I became pregnant, but soon after miscarried. We continued on with fertility treatments and ended our quest once we attempted an adoption. Although we never did have children, Ken and I have accepted our fate and moved on. Our marriage remains strong, which both of us attribute our accomplishment to having successfully resolved our "having children issue." Even though we never had children, Ken considers it a success because he and I were able to try and were able to learn how to communicate with each other about anything.

What Worked:
+ Ken and I were able to openly communicate with each other and move forward despite the fact that we started out our relationship with a big misunderstanding. I thought Ken would get a vasovasostomy and Ken had no recollection of ever making that commitment. However, he believes that he may have once said that he was open to considering it and I talked myself into believing that this was his "commitment."
+ I worked with Ken to resolve his fears of being a poor father by taking care of my niece and nephew. Although I planned the weekend poorly, I did show Ken that I cared enough to try.
+ I introduced Ken to another couple that had successfully undergone the same process that we were considering. Ken learned the

pros and cons of vasovasostomies and was exposed to a positive image of a man after the ordeal.

+ We communicated with empathy and agreed to talk about our differences twice a month. Even though Ken was putting stops in place for his decision, he agreed to talk about our problem.

+ Ken and I continued to communicate until we resolved our differences. Ken agreed to get a reverse vasectomy, allowing me the opportunity to have children. This intense process brought closure to our problem.

What Didn't Work:

+ Ken shrugged off responsibility by letting me continue to believe that he would consider getting a reversal. What exactly does "considering" getting a reversal mean? It means a lot of thought about the procedure, including recollection of how painful the vasectomy may have been in the first place. Result: procrastination.

+ Seeing the wrong kind of therapist did not help. This experience further convinced Ken and me that we were truly in this alone. (This is discussed further in Chapter 11).

+ Ken's decision to get a vasovasostomy would have been better if he had been convinced that becoming a father was truly what he wanted, rather than doing this merely to please me.

Analysis

The desire to have children ran deeply within me, almost as deeply as my love for Ken. During the courtship phase, and all phases of a marriage or a committed relationship, these types of desires need to be clearly communicated and subsequent actions, if any, need to be completely understood. By setting ground rules for discussions early, we were able to maximize our effectiveness and stop disagreements before they got out of hand. My attempts at exposing Ken to parenting and vasovasostomies were mixed. The practice parenting set the process back several months by putting Ken in the middle of a weekend for which he had no preparation.

But introducing Ken to another man who had had a reversal and was willing to answer all of the intimate questions about the process ended a lot of Ken's fears.

Once Ken and I had overcome the rocky start and reached agreement, we showed the maturity that our relationship had acquired. Successfully resolving the process of deciding to have children was what we considered our win. Although we wished we had been blessed with a child, we are happy that we resolved the process together and that we are now stronger as a couple than before.

By being able to reach a satisfying conclusion to a conflict as serious as this one, we believe that we can conquer anything together.

For those of you considering a vasovasostomy, we suggest that you contact a urologist who performs vasovasostomies as a specialty and ask if he or she could refer you to someone who has been through the procedure. Finding a couple on your own with this circumstance may be difficult. Prior to undergoing this procedure, <u>both</u> partners should be checked for virility of their fertility.

This chapter opened with a statistic that only 5 percent of vasectomies are reversed. For your partner to agree to undergo this operation, it will involve a lot of soul searching on his part, and an acceptance that his life will be significantly changed. You will need to examine your finances to see that you can afford the procedure, and, ideally, he will have accepted the idea that his life will benefit from children. Good luck! You will need it with this one.

Here's a summary of Ken's advice for those select men to remember once they've decided to undo the ties that bind them:

1. Don't do anything until you've confirmed that she's fertile. Think about how stupid you'll feel if she isn't, and you undergo the procedure and find you two can't have kids anyhow.

2. Get a good doctor. Ask lots of questions about success rates, costs, and what to expect. Do you trust this person with the family jewels?

3. Don't tell anyone at work what you're doing (other than possibly your boss). The last thing you want when you're recovering is a bunch of guys snickering in the background while you're hunting for an ice pack, or a bunch of women telling you how brave and "sensitive" you are. People are going to notice that you are walking funny and will want to know what's going on. Tell them it's a groin pull from moving a refrigerator.

4. If the doctor tells you not to do something for four weeks after surgery, OBEY!!! This is not the time to be macho. Oh, and wear your "scrotum tote-em" (athletic supporter) for as long as your doctor tells you.

5. Make your wife pamper you for a few days. Have her rent all your favorite videos. Catch up on the Stallone movies that she never wanted to watch with you. Eat your favorite junk foods. She won't dare hassle you after what you've been through.

6. Be gentle the first time you try anything with your wife. It's still sore down there. Expect the first, and possibly the second and third, ejaculation to be red from leftover blood. Those who have been through this strongly suggest that you not try for three times in the first afternoon.

7. If the reversal is a success . . . enjoy. If it's not . . . enjoy. You tried.

Chapter 9

Agreeing Not to Have Children

Y ou have concluded, for various reasons, that you absolutely do not want children. Perhaps you had a bad childhood, you may think you're too old, you may believe that you cannot afford children, or you simply don't want to give up your freedom. Reaching this conclusion does not make you an oddball or a social outcast. In fact, childless couples have received increased social acceptance paralleling an increasing number of couples who either cannot have children due to fertility issues, or who have decided not to have children.

A 2002 United States Census Bureau statistics report found that almost 20 percent of women and couples are childless, up from 10.2 percent in 1979.[1] Study data included women age forty to forty-four, an age range that includes the statistical end of childbearing.

The reasons for opting not to have children range from physical to psychological. Physical reasons include easier access to birth control, waiting longer to marry, and personal health of mother and child. Some couples have debilitating genes or genetic diseases such as cystic fibrosis, muscular dystrophy, and Huntington's chorea that they do not want to pass on to their children. Other women find that their health may be adversely affected by becoming pregnant and giving birth. This is especially true for women with diabetes. Some women find they have infertility problems that do not allow them to bear children. A 1995 survey revealed that 6.1 million women between the ages of fifteen and forty-four experienced infertility problems.[2]

Psychological reasons for not having children stem from the higher rates of divorce and separation among couples. Women are becoming more apprehensive about raising a child as a single parent. They may decline having children because they want an education, a career, and financial stability. A person raised in a large family is more inclined to want a large family. A person raised in a small family or as a single child is more likely to have a small family or opt not to have children at all.

If you marry with the agreement not to have children, it's possible that at least one of you will change your mind, and that will certainly affect your relationship. Change is inevitable in life and your decision to have children most likely will change in some way over time.

Many people who originally agreed not to have children decide that they can no longer go through life without children. Some experience a change in their relationship or a remarriage that brings the desire to have a family. Some women respond to their biological clocks, realizing they really do want children. Others experience an improved financial situation that allows for the family they felt they could not have previously. Some simply respond to their new desire to have a family, feeling that children will complete the marriage. These urges *do* happen and people *do* change their minds about children.

Remember Allan and Dianne from Chapter 1 (see page 11)? When they married, Dianne thought she could live a full life without children, but that changed a year later when she was struck by the maternal urge. She tried to talk with her husband for two years about wanting to have a family. In the end, Dianne left her husband and became pregnant by artificial insemination through a sperm donor. She's happier now; unfortunately changing her decision to have children cost her her marriage.

This is a classic example of how people find their opinions changing with age. At thirty-eight, Dianne honestly felt she didn't want children; at thirty-nine, the deep desire for a baby or her maternal instinct, a very basic human drive, surfaced. She could not let go of her desire, so she sacrificed her marriage to become a mother. Who suffered from her decision? Obviously her marriage suffered. But her unborn child may also suffer from not having the opportunity to grow up in a two-parent household.

What if you're on the fence about wanting children and you're dating a man who doesn't want children? How committed are both of you about remaining child-free? These are questions that need to be addressed.

Rachael is thirty-four and currently dating a man who doesn't want to have children due to health and financial concerns. She keeps wavering back and forth on the issue of children for various reasons, but mainly due to her marital status and finances. For years, Rachael has known that she wants either four kids or no kids and has even toyed with the thought of adoption. She has been dating her boyfriend for eight months and is very emotionally involved with him.

If Rachael decides not to have children and remains with her current boyfriend, she may have regrets that she will need to deal with and that may take years to heal. If she decides that she wants children, then she and her boyfriend need to open up their communication and explore each other's goals and needs. They will want to follow the advice in Part I, Chapters 2 and 3, and may also want to take Planned Parenthood's Parenting Questionnaire in the appendix.

If you decide that you want to be child-free, how will you ensure that your desire is fulfilled? Discuss your wish to remain child-free with your partner. How does he feel? Can you honestly go through life without children? How committed are both of you to remaining child-free? These questions need to be addressed with conviction.

Nancy and Chris are in complete agreement not to have or adopt children. For a number of reasons, each independently made the decision not to have children. As a result, the decision on children has never been an issue in their marriage. They've never debated or discussed this issue at great length.

When asked to share some of the reasons they decided not to have children, Nancy and Chris both talked about their childhoods.

Nancy's parents came from large families and were raised in extreme poverty. Her mother was one of fifteen children and did not graduate from high school. Nancy's father was one of nine children and had two or three years of technical training. When Nancy was twelve, her mother told her, "The only advice my mother gave me when I got married was to have only two kids. I followed that advice. If I had it to do over again, I wouldn't have gotten married and had children." Nancy concluded from this that both her grandmother and her mother felt that having a large family was a burden to women.

Nancy's mother was not a nurturing woman. Her father had been an alcoholic, and she suffered poor economic and educational circumstances—because of all this, Nancy's mother had an unhappy, stressed childhood. Her ability to relate warmly to Nancy and Nancy's brother was limited. Nancy's mother did not present a positive picture of marriage or of motherhood. Nancy's subjective understanding is that her mother felt like a victim trapped in those roles.

Consequently, Nancy developed a dislike of being around babies and younger children. She only babysat twice as a teenager, and that was because she was forced to babysit for an aunt. She remembers a huge relief when her babysitting nights were over.

Due to both of her parents' large families, reunions were enormous— filled with four generations of babies and great-great-grandmothers. Family socializing was largely segregated by sex, with the women entertaining one another as part of the food preparation process and after dinner at the table. The conversation was often related to children—sickness, walking, talking, and other baby-related activities that bored Nancy. She always considered herself intellectually curious—and babies didn't stimulate her.

Chris, Nancy's husband, is the youngest of seven children. His parents divorced when he was eleven, and this was very traumatic for him. As a result, he began drinking as a young teenager, became an alcoholic by his mid-twenties, and experimented with recreational drugs as well. Fortunately, he entered a recovery program in his mid-thirties and has been sober and drug-free for more than seven years. Although Chris likes children, he feels that his addiction issues set his life back. He doesn't have the required financial resources to have children, and he feels that he does not have the energy to raise a family. He says that if he were ten to fifteen years younger he would consider children.

A silently angry mother with poor coping mechanisms was not a good role model for Nancy. Childhood experiences have much to do with how we live our lives, our ambitions, our prejudices, and other defining character traits. Nancy's family experiences have had a deep impact on her life and on how she perceives potential family life and herself as a mother. As most of her memorable impressions are negative, she has created an enormous barrier that blocks her from wanting to become a mother. If Nancy were to have a child (without first reconciling her childhood issues), she would most likely repeat the same rearing patterns as her mother, and cause similar problems for her own child.

Alison also does not want to have children, but her reasons are much different. Alison is single and thirty-four years old. Everyone where she works has children, and she's always feeling pressured to have children by friends and family and work associates. Since her early twenties, Alison has not had the urge to have a baby and she doesn't think she ever will.

Alison had a great childhood and was one of two children. She babysits often and finds children a joy to be around. She is excited when she is around a child and he grasps something new. But after four hours, she's ready to give the kids back to their parents.

From the first date, Alison is up-front and honest about not wanting children. She believes that this protects her from getting emotionally involved with someone who doesn't share her feelings. She gets varied reactions. Some are curious and ask why she doesn't want children, some respect her decision, some are turned off, and some are honest and tell her that they do want children.

Alison is happy with who she is. She's content not being married, likes her lifestyle with the freedom to travel, saves money for things she wants, and likes not having to be responsible for another person. Through babysitting, Alison feels she has the best of both worlds; she can enjoy children and still enjoy her freedom. Being child-free seems to work for Alison. Perhaps her thoughts on having children will change in the next four to six years when she is closer to the end of her fertile period. Or maybe her thoughts will change if she enters into a fulfilling, well-adjusted relationship.

Depending on age, choice in birth control may also change. For example, a woman under the age of thirty who feels she does not want children usually considers temporary birth control options. These include birth control pills, an IUD, a diaphragm, the Patch, injections, and condoms. After all, for a woman under the age of thirty, *no* to having children now can still mean *maybe* or *yes* to having children later.

A woman who is absolutely certain she does not want to produce any offspring usually considers a permanent form of birth control such as a hysterectomy or tubal ligation, or the vasectomy of her partner. Interestingly, one-third of tubal ligations are performed on unmarried women (women for whom the vasectomy of a partner is not an option). In addition, tubal ligations are two times more common than vasectomies. An article entitled "Women, Men, and Contraceptive Sterilization," in the May 2000 issue of *Fertility and Sterility*, reported that the highest percentage of tubal ligations are performed within one year of a woman's last wanted birth.[3] These numbers indicate that more women will choose permanent birth control than men.

How many of these women have regrets about their choice of permanent sterilization? A 1995 study by the National Center for Chronic Disease Prevention and Health Promotion, found that 25 percent of women who had tubal ligations expressed a desire (either her own desire, her partner's desire, or both) to have the operation reversed.[4] Likewise, about 11 percent of women who were cohabitating or married to a partner with a vasectomy voiced their desire for him to get a reversal.[5] The most common reasons for men to change their minds about their procedure were that they were too young at the time of the original operation to realize they may want children in the future, and that they didn't realize how much a new relationship and changes in lifestyle and finances would affect their desire for children.

If you've had surgery as your choice of birth control, and now find yourself changing your mind, here are some options you may want to consider:

+ **Tubal ligation reversal.** Cost is out-of-pocket for the patient, which means it's not covered by insurance, and the price ranges between $10,000 and $18,000. Women must be under the age of forty and must qualify for the procedure. Pregnancy success rates are 70 percent to 90 percent, and there is an increased risk of ectopic pregnancy (tubal pregnancy) following a tubal ligation reversal.[6]

+ **Vasovasostomy.** A vasovasostomy costs between $4,000 and $20,000 and is not covered by insurance.[7] The success rate of having live sperm in the ejaculate after the reversal is around 90 percent.[8] The success rate of the reversal tends to decline when the time period between the vasectomy and the reversal is fifteen years or greater.

+ **In vitro fertilization (IVF).** IVF is not covered by insurance; depending on the complexity of your needs, costs can range from $7,500 to $12,000 per procedure. You must qualify for the IVF program, which is dependent on health and age. Success rates vary and there is an increased probability of multiple births.[9]

+ **Adoption** can cost $8,000 to $30,000 and the waiting period can be between two months to three years or more.[10] (See Chapter 16 for more about adoption.)

♦ **Nurturing can come in many forms.** Although not a replacement for a child, a pet (especially a puppy or kitten) can fill some of your nurturing needs. Pets cost less, don't talk, and may be easier to train than children! Pets are wonderful companions that can give you unconditional love and provide similar challenges of having young children.

There are a number of couples and single people who are content to be child-free. Many child-free adults (like Alison on page 109) genuinely like children; they simply do not want children of their own. They are pleased with their lifestyles, careers, responsibilities, incomes, and relationships. If you are in a relationship in which you have agreed not to have children, our only word of advice is to be true to your decision.

For those of you who have actively chosen to be child-free and are seeking support and information, you can visit an online organization at *www.nokidding.net*. This site focuses on various ways to support your child-free lifestyle.

Chapter 10

Becoming Pregnant Against His Wishes

D on't do it! Regardless of her age, when a woman has an unplanned pregnancy, the man she is involved with often casts judgment, accusing her of tricking him into fatherhood and hoping for commitment if one isn't already there. When a woman is being deceptive about birth control, she is risking severe consequences, not only for her relationship but for the unborn child as well.

Common reasons a woman will deliberately become pregnant without the consent of her partner include the following:

1. She is tired of waiting for her partner to commit to marriage.
2. She is fed up with postponing a family and doesn't feel she can wait any longer.
3. She thinks a baby will help save her marriage.

4. She thinks she can change her partner's mind about having children by becoming pregnant.
5. She is selfish in her desire for a baby.

Whatever the reason for becoming pregnant without his consent, there is no guarantee that a man will remain committed to the relationship just because his partner is having his baby.

Dr. Kovacs has found that in relationships with unplanned pregnancies, or pregnancies without mutual agreement, the couple tends to experience an increase in stress, conflict, resentment, betrayal, distrust, and an overall deterioration in communication. All of these compounding factors can easily lead to separation or divorce.

Accidents Do Happen

An unintended pregnancy is usually the result of birth control failure, the rhythm method is off, or the misuse of a birth control apparatus. If the birth control produces a surprise pregnancy, the relationship does not suffer directly from the pregnancy. The couple accepts that there was a failure in their contraceptive choice. In situations like this, many couples move forward and face their consequences responsibly. Accidents do happen; they accept that and address the situation.

The rhythm method does work for some women, but they need to have regular cycles and to track their charts with constant vigilance. Their partners also have to abstain during peak fertility days. So, the rhythm method all too easily can produce an "oops" child. The birth control pill, a popular option, is between 92 percent and 99.7 percent effective, which means accidents can happen.[1] Surprisingly, constant breastfeeding is up to 98 percent effective as a birth control method, but only if the woman hasn't had a period since delivery and has the baby suckle on both breasts every four hours, or uses a breast pump.[2] The drawback is that this method is only effective for six months. There are condoms that are 85 to

98 percent effective, female condoms that are 79 to 95 percent effective, and spermicides that are 71 to 85 percent effective. These options give you a 2 to 29 percent chance of producing a surprise baby.

Birth control choices in the 99 percent plus range include the Ring (Nuvaring), the Patch (Ortho Evra), and the Shot (Depo-Provera). For more information on contraceptive choices you can visit *www.planned parenthood.org*.

Conception by Deception

Let's take a closer look at intended versus unintended pregnancies. A woman getting pregnant without her partner's consent is an intended pregnancy conceived deliberately and with the full knowledge of one participating partner—in this case, the woman. Tracy Quan, a freelance writer, coined the term "conception by deception" to describe the one-sided decision to become pregnant.[3] Under these circumstances, often the woman has deceived her partner by giving him a false impression they were having protected sex. When conception occurs under these conditions, the outcome can vary widely.

Some men will end the relationship, others will demand their partner get an abortion, and some will "do the right thing" even though they feel duped. None of these options are optimal and all are damaging to the relationship. If the relationship continues, the man will frequently harbor feelings of betrayal toward the woman and perhaps even toward their child. He may feel he can no longer trust his partner to follow through with personal agreements. To make matters worse, this lack of trust can extend into other areas of the relationship, which often continues to deteriorate to the point of destruction.

Women who secretly plan a pregnancy are playing Russian roulette with their relationships. The odds of a favorable outcome are not in their favor, but, as long as there are enough men who make the best of the situation, there will be women who think they have a chance of succeeding. For most women, having a baby through trickery usually does not get them the results that they hoped for, as was the case for Larry and Brenda.

Larry and Brenda had been dating for two years. They had talked about marriage, but there was still no engagement ring and no set wedding date. Brenda was anxious about their relationship and wanted to force their informal engagement into a marriage commitment by getting pregnant. So, without confronting Larry, she stopped taking her birth control pills and shortly thereafter became pregnant. Larry had always intended to marry Brenda, but now he felt pressured into making both a marriage commitment and a commitment to become a father much sooner than he had expected. He had plans to buy a house first, move into management at work, and become more financially stable before starting a family. Brenda's unexpected pregnancy would delay his dreams, but Brenda would get her wish of having a wedding and a baby.

Just three weeks before the wedding, while Brenda was in the first trimester of her pregnancy, she lost the baby. Larry consoled her, but he was secretly relieved. Over the ensuing three weeks, all Brenda could do was focus on wanting to get pregnant as soon as possible. Larry felt used, believing that all she wanted was his sperm without any regard to his future plans. They argued and the wedding was called off three days before it was scheduled to take place. Within a year of breaking up with Larry, Brenda married another man and had a baby with him. The experience left Larry wary of women and their intentions.

Analysis

There was an obvious lack of communication between Larry and Brenda that left Brenda feeling insecure about the future of their relationship. Brenda felt the need to force their relationship to the next level of commitment through pregnancy. Her secret plot and deceptive actions destroyed any trust that she and Larry had built over their two-year relationship. Not only did she show disrespect for Larry and their relationship, but she also displayed a lack of regard for the security of her unborn child—there was no guarantee that Brenda wouldn't end up an unwed, single parent. Perhaps Brenda was suffering from an unconscious compulsion to have a child, something that will not be satisfied by a second pregnancy with another man. Brenda needs to evaluate her drive to have a child and ensure that her desire for a baby is for the right reasons.

Larry, in turn, did not reveal to Brenda that he felt "used" and taken advantage of. He assumed that Brenda knew he was committed to the relationship. Unfortunately, they did not share their dreams and goals with each other nor did they talk about their future as a couple (except for a few brief hints about marriage). This left each assuming that the other understood the future of their relationship. As a result, Brenda felt that Larry needed a little urging, such as a pregnancy, to accelerate a wedding ceremony. Had Brenda and Larry been more open with each other they may have experienced a different outcome. Larry could have communicated his timetable and it might have been fine with Brenda. Open communication is vital to the success of a relationship.

Jennifer is thirty-five and unmarried. Because she was an unwanted child, she doesn't plan to ever have children. Her father never wanted to have children and said as much when he married Jennifer's mother. The marriage wasn't stable, so Jennifer's mom got pregnant to keep her husband from leaving her. It worked, at least, for a little while. He stayed until Jennifer was three and then left the two of them on their own.

Jennifer has always felt that she was the one to blame because she didn't do her job, which was to keep her father from leaving. The experience has been very difficult for her. She has trouble sustaining healthy relationships and doesn't experience much happiness.

Jennifer still harbors anger toward her parents. She feels the world would be better off if people would deal with their issues in a responsible fashion before bringing a child into the picture.

Analysis

This is a classic example of how having a child to save your marriage has a negative impact on the innocent child. When a husband is not interested in having children of his own, and his wife uses a pregnancy to hold the man in an unstable marriage, the relationship is doomed. Jennifer's father clearly said that he did not want children, yet when the marriage was falling apart, her mother got pregnant. For Jennifer and her family, this was a no-win situation. Jennifer's father felt betrayed and no longer trusted his wife. As a result, Jennifer and her mother were abandoned, leaving Jennifer with deep emotional scars. Not only is she enraged at her absent father, she is angry with her mother for her selfish reason for having a baby.

Until she comes to terms with her unresolved issues concerning her parents and their divorce, it appears that Jennifer will continue to be affected by actions that took place thirty-five years ago. Due to her deep emotional scars, if Jennifer ever has children, she could extend this cycle, allowing the child to believe he or she is responsible for the success or failure of a marriage, to any offspring she may have in the future.

In Jennifer's example, the entire family suffered the consequences. The marriage dissolved, Jennifer's father abandoned her, and she appears to have suffered the most from the effects of her mother's deception.

Some women hope that by getting pregnant, their partner will feel an immediate bond with the unborn baby and will end up wanting to have children as well. This is hardly ever the case.

Janet and Andrew were gridlocked after four years of discussions on children. Andrew had absolutely no desire to raise a child. His parents had divorced when he was young, and he spent a lot of time helping his mother raise his four sisters. From the time he was fifteen, he had wanted to get a vasectomy, but he never expressed this to Janet. When he did talk about the possibility of an operation, Janet would always tell him that would end the relationship.

Janet thought that she could change Andrew's mind by secretly getting pregnant. But when she did, Andrew didn't change his stance; their emotions caused escalating arguments. Soon afterward, Janet got an abortion. Andrew loved Janet and wanted to spend the rest of his life with her but felt emotionally blackmailed. Their relationship could not withstand the strain and they broke up. A few weeks later, Andrew made an appointment to get a vasectomy. Andrew said that when Janet learned of his vasectomy, she was completely surprised. This made him realize how strongly Janet had convinced herself that he wanted children.

Analysis

Secrets are disastrous for relationships. Not only did Janet not tell Andrew about her intense wish to have a child, but Andrew also did not reveal how long he had wanted to get the vasectomy. Obviously, Janet and Andrew were not expressing themselves clearly and openly, and they also were not listening to each other. Using a pregnancy to hold on to a marriage is definitely blackmail, and this is harmful for everyone involved, especially the child. This couple had a constellation of dysfunctional behaviors: inadequate communication including secretiveness, withholding information, reliance on "mind reading," and ineffective arguments.

The big question is why did Janet decide to get an abortion after all the time she spent wanting to have a baby?

This couple could have carried out a trial separation with a couples' therapist to work on communicating, exploring past history, and listening to each other, and resolving their individual issues about marriage and family. Whether a couple divorces or stays together, these issues must be resolved if they are to have any kind of fulfilling relationship.

Molly and Robert got married in their mid-twenties after a two-year courtship. They hadn't really talked about children prior to marriage, and Molly felt that children would just be a natural progression. Robert never actually verbalized that he didn't want children. A year after they married, when Molly became pregnant, Robert voiced his disapproval and asked her to get an abortion. Molly was devastated, but she agreed; an action that she has regretted with every passing anniversary of the procedure. Five years have gone by; Robert and Molly are still married, and now have a one-year-old daughter whom both of them wanted.

Analysis

Abortion should not be considered a form of birth control. Unfortunately for some, it is. Clearly Molly and Robert needed to improve their communication. Had they discussed and shared their goals and the timing of when they wanted to start a family, they may have avoided the heartache of an abortion. Many women who choose to have an abortion will experience depression for years afterward and require therapy.

Sometimes when a man agrees to have children with his partner, he isn't being truthful to his emotions. When this happens, the couple experiences similar issues and problems as couples who find themselves confronting an unplanned pregnancy. When Linda, thirty-seven, wanted a baby, her husband, Ben (in his forties), agreed to it only because he wanted to make her happy. They needed fertility help. At the consultation visit, Linda said they would go through with artificial insemination. Ben agreed unenthusiastically. He participated in the process, helped pick out a sperm donor, and accompanied Linda to the appointments. She got pregnant and gave birth to a baby boy. After the son was born, Ben started distancing himself. He worked longer hours and found other excuses not to be at home. In spite of this, the couple had a second baby, this time a girl, via the same procedure. Afterwards, Ben distanced himself even more. Linda was ecstatic with children; he was happy that she was happy, but he was not truly happy.

Analysis

The myth that one person's happiness can make another person happy is certainly at work in this situation. Unfortunately, Ben did not reveal his true feelings, resentment, or anger, choosing to suppress them.

Linda was not very perceptive about what was going on in her husband's mind. She may have been so wrapped up in the children that she missed the cues her husband was giving when he worked late and put distance between them. Any sort of critical event in this family will set off a huge explosion. By suppressing his emotions, Ben also risks physical disorders, such as high blood pressure, stomach problems, or whatever he is genetically predisposed to develop.

Becoming pregnant against your partner's wishes is not a game. Having your partner's child does not guarantee that he will remain in the relationship. You are dealing with serious emotional consequences that affect all parties involved: your partner, you, and your unborn child. Often, the innocent child suffers the most with abandonment and rejection issues, heavy emotional scars that he or she carries forever. For this reason alone, women should never consider pregnancy as an option to get a man to commit to marriage or to become a father before he is ready.

Open communication and the expression of wants and desires can help prevent heartache, unnecessary surgery, and unwanted pregnancies.

You may be pleasantly surprised with your outcome.

Chapter 11

Getting Outside Help

*W*hen difficulties arise, and you find that you and your partner are no longer making progress, seek outside help through a third-party facilitator. In most cases, therapists are qualified and better equipped to guide you through the decision to have children or to remain childless. Finding the right counselor for this specific problem is important. Look for a licensed professional such as a marriage and family therapist (M.F.T.), nurse psychotherapist, clinical social worker (C.S.W.), or a clinical psychologist trained in family dynamics and family therapy. These professionals will have experience in the area of family planning and conflict resolution and can assist with these monumental decisions. Any therapist can assist you with communication skills by teaching you an approach that has structure—you can use this as a container for your emotions and reactions as you move forward in your decision-making process.

Going to a therapist for the first time can be intimidating and embarrassing. We all need others at critical times. If you and your partner have reached a stalemate or are in an explosive position that is destroying your marriage, you need help. The first step in finding the right therapist is to try to find someone you know—your doctor, a friend, or a clergy member—who can recommend a good fit.

If that doesn't work, look up your local M.F.T. association online by going to the American Association for Marriage and Family Therapy (*www.aamft.org*) or look in your phone book. Each professional association will have a referral services listing.

You should screen your therapist. Regardless of how you find the therapist, you and your partner will need to be comfortable with the person. You will be disclosing your innermost secrets, desires, and concerns. Keep this in mind when you ask questions of your potential therapist.

Interview the therapist over the phone or in person through a consultation visit. Don't be shy about asking questions. If the therapist isn't able to ease this process, then you probably don't have a good fit. Questions to ask include the following:

1. Are you licensed?
2. How long have you been practicing?
3. How much experience do you have in assisting couples to resolve conflict when one partner wants a child and the other one doesn't?
4. How do you approach this type of issue?
5. What is your success rate among couples with this predicament?
6. What type of exercises will you assign between appointments?
7. Do you have any biases or restrictions regarding religion, unwed couples, or family planning issues?
8. In general, how many sessions does it take to resolve conflict in this area?
9. What do you charge per session and do you accept insurance?

10. How soon can you see me and my partner?
11. Do you make house calls? (Ask this if it's more convenient for you.)

A licensed M.F.T. will have at least a master's degree with an additional 3,000 hours of supervised experience, and will have the following initials after his or her name: L.M.F.T. or M.F.T. These initials indicate that the person is licensed and his or her license will be prominently displayed in the office. In addition to the master's degree, many therapists also have a doctoral degree or Ph.D. In California, M.F.T.s and other professional therapists are required to put their license numbers in their advertisements, on their business cards, etc.

Look for a therapist with three or more years' experience and a high degree of success resolving conflict between couples. Therapists will often see the couple separately. Some therapists such as Dr. Kovacs prefer to see the couple together, then individually, and then together again. This forum allows the therapist to understand each individual and the issue(s) at hand before attempting to treat the couple. For some couples, this approach works well because it reduces anxiety in the session, helps improve communication, and strengthens the relationship

Each partner will be instructed to complete weekly assignments between sessions, which will assist in resolving their dilemma. The six basic tools that a marriage therapist will use include:

1. Communication
2. Problem solving
3. Conflict resolution
4. Negotiating
5. Building empathy
6. Forgiveness

The primary underpinning for all these tools, and of interpersonal relationships as well, is communication, commonly defined as giving and exchanging information. Communication includes nonverbal language, or body language—gestures, facial expressions, and posture—as well as thoughts and feelings. A rule of communication theory is a person cannot *not* communicate. Even silence is communication.

The therapist will examine what each partner brings to the marriage from his or her own families and childhoods and how it affects the relationship today. These marriage therapists use a developmental framework and theories. They approach your situation by looking at your developmental process—what occurred during your childhood, adolescence, and early adulthood. Research supports that if some family dynamics issues are not resolved earlier in life, they are often repeated in the marriage. Resolving those issues with a therapist will improve your marriage and fulfill your dreams and goals as a couple.

The therapist you choose should be supportive of your religious beliefs and partnership preference whether you are married or living with your partner, and should not show any bias toward your family planning issues. If you feel that partiality in any of these areas conflicts with your beliefs, find another counselor. If you are dissatisfied with one therapist, find one who better suits your personality. If the therapist is a professional, you won't be hurting his or her feelings if you go to someone else. Remember, the therapist is working for you.

Resolving conflict on whether to have children can take time; this process should not be rushed. Many couples complete therapy in an average of ten to twelve sessions, seeing their therapist once a week, or bimonthly. However, each couple and individual in the relationship is unique, with varying layers of experiences that have affected their positions on children. The length of time required to resolve issues varies with each couple. So, be patient, do your homework, and above all, stick with your program until you have reached your goal of attaining an amicable agreement on children!

Marriage and family therapist rates range from $45 to $200 per session, with an average cost of about $95. You can expect to pay $450 to $2,400 by the time you complete therapy. Considering the importance of this decision to your relationship, it's a bargain.

Most insurance providers do not pay for marital counseling, unless you or your spouse is in crisis or suffering severe emotional distress. Certainly, a couple at an impasse in resolving a difficult issue, such as that of whether to have children, will be considered appropriate for therapeutic intervention.

There are varying degrees of emotional and mental distress, from crises and situational disturbances to major psychiatric disorders. Your professional therapist will be able to diagnose and treat your concerns and problems with respect, care, and knowledge. Rest assured that your sessions will be treated with the utmost confidentiality. No one has access to your records without your permission. Although the therapist will submit claim forms with a diagnostic category to your insurance company, these records are all confidential.

If your therapist is billing your insurance to assist you in overcoming your conflict on children, in most cases you will be diagnosed with a situational problem or a crisis. Crises are normal, and everyone has a crisis when change, a serious illness, a loss, or an accident occurs. Childbirth, children leaving home, getting a job, being laid off, retiring are all developmental transitions that can cause crises for people. Most marital problems such as separation, divorce, remarriage, and conflict over children are considered situational disturbances. These events, along with clients who suffer from anxiety and depression, are the most frequent kinds of problems seen in private practice.

When you find yourself reaching for the phone to call a therapist to assist you and your partner, you have reached a critical point in your relationship and it calls for immediate attention. A good therapist will try to schedule you within a day or two of your call.

Another option in keeping the cost down while resolving your conflict is to use an Employee Assisted Program (EAP). Many companies provide employees with EAPs to support their well-being. Fees are around $500 per year per employee (often paid by the employer), confidentiality is assured, and there are no additional charges to family members. Some services offered in the EAPs include work-related counseling, anger management, substance abuse intervention and assessment, marital/family counseling, and individual counseling. EAP visits are limited to three to six sessions, and many EAP therapists serve in crisis counseling centers that focus on substance abuse and behavioral disorders. However, many therapists in private practice provide EAP sessions, and then switch to regular insurance services if you are covered.

Ken and I agreed that our differences on wanting to have children were bigger than we could handle on our own. In our long, futile attempt, we had exhausted each other, but we had not fallen out of love. We wanted to save our marriage, so we made the decision to go to counseling and chose a confidential EAP program offered through my company. Our first red flag (which we did not recognize at the time): It took three weeks before we could be seen.

When asked what brought us to counseling, I quickly responded that we were having difficulty in deciding to have children, elaborating that Ken was opposed to the idea and that I eagerly wanted to have a child. Surprisingly, the therapist replied, "Oh, is that all your problem is?"

We were shocked at her response. We immediately felt we were in the wrong office. Stunned, I responded, "Yes, but this is a monumental problem. It could lead to divorce if we can't come to a consensus. We love each other very much and we believe in marriage. I don't want Ken changing his mind just to appease me. This is a very serious issue for us and we need help."

I seemed to have gotten the therapist's attention because she focused the rest of our time on obtaining background information. She covered the usual preliminary work: how long we had been married, how we met, how long we'd known each other before marrying, my knowledge of Ken's vasectomy, our professions, our ages, and why we felt the way we did about having children of our own. During the fact-gathering phase, Ken didn't like that the therapist couldn't remember my name. After an hour, and without summarizing our concerns or personal progress, the therapist scheduled another appointment for the following week.

Unfortunately, Ken and I did not have a positive first impression of our therapist. Neither of us was even partially satisfied with our experience, but we reluctantly agreed it was probably best to continue rather than to find someone else. We thought that if we changed therapists, we would have to go through the same initial introductory process again, which would prolong our decision-making process. In hindsight, changing over to a marriage counselor or an infertility counselor would have been better for us. After our second counseling appointment, Ken and I concluded we needed somebody more qualified for our specific problem if we were going to make progress.

Julie and Tim (see Chapter 4, pages 40–43) took their differences about children to a marriage family therapist after they realized they were at a stalemate. Prior to their marriage, Julie and Tim's minister noticed that the couple did not see eye-to-eye on the issue of children and recommended that they talk more on the subject or seek out counseling. Julie had initially agreed not to have children, but a couple of years after they married Julie began to seriously want children. Tim thought the issue had been resolved before their marriage and refused to talk about it further, but Julie convinced Tim to see a counselor with her.

They selected a counselor through the phone book. After their first appointment, they realized they didn't like him and didn't go back. Driven to work on resolving their problem, Julie asked for a referral from a practicing psychiatrist friend who provided her with the name of a therapist who had clinical counseling skills. This second counselor had worked on two cases similar to Julie and Tim's, so she was familiar with how to treat them. During the first session, they connected with this new therapist, who used various exercises to help the couple overcome issues, enabling them to move forward and eventually, four months later, come to an amicable decision to have children.

Analysis

Julie and Tim displayed commitment to resolving their issues and saving their marriage. They sought out another counselor when they realized their first counselor was not a good fit. Then, with professional guidance, they completed exercises that helped them overcome elements that had been preventing them from making progress on their own. As a result, they strengthened their marriage and both realized, with equal desire, that they wanted a family.

Marriage counselors can provide you with an objective forum for working out your problems. Many marriage counselors are excellent, and if you and your partner work well with your counselor, he or she can streamline your decision-making process. A good counselor will help by breaking down the communication barriers, finding the real problem, and keeping the focus on the problem. If you decide to go this route, the benefits of counseling can be outstanding. The number-one benefit is improved communication. You'll also learn how to solve problems together. Counseling can help couples learn to be friends again, learn to date again, and learn the importance of taking twenty minutes every day to talk with each other about how each person's day was.

Part III

Outcomes

Chapter 12

The Key to a Satisfying Relationship: Communication

C ouples who have gone through a decision-making process communicating as a team, and who have succeeded with a mutually gratifying agreement to have or not to have children, tend to have more satisfying relationships. A study conducted by Virginia P. Richmond, James C. McCroskey, and K. David Roach examined couples in these types of situations. They found that the couples communicate in a coactive style, sharing the responsibility of their decision.[1] Their agreement on a life-altering decision has brought harmony into their lives, and the level of stress and anxiety they experienced before the decision is now relieved. In a way, they have mapped out their future as a couple and can now move forward with their lives with greater confidence that they can face whatever challenges lie ahead. This doesn't mean, of course, that being able to agree on whether to have children is the only determining factor for a happy marriage.

According to Dr. John Gottman, coauthor of *The Seven Principles for Making Marriage Work* (Three Rivers Press, 1999), the success of a relationship is based on how differences and areas of conflict are resolved as a couple. Those who approach their issues in a calm, nonthreatening manner often have more success reaching a resolution than couples who begin their discussions with anger.[2]

After going through this decision-making process and reaching a consensus on children, many couples have improved their communication abilities. They have learned how to communicate more effectively. As a couple, they now know how to identify the root problem in a conflict, what to do, what not to do, and when to discuss their differences for optimal results. In addition, they know how to structure their conversations to have the best chance for a fruitful discussion.

Ken and I resolved our differences on children. We believe we have grown much more as a couple. Ken says, "I would like to think that my bending on the 'baby thing' wasn't the reason for this benefit. I honestly think we would have worked out our differences either way the decision went because we shared the problem equally."

Through improved communication and joint decision-making, you and your partner will have a better understanding of each other and a more pleasing relationship. Sharing with each other your childhood experiences, goals, dreams, and wishes allows each of you to understand how your partner feels and why. You may not necessarily agree with each other's aspirations or timing, but you will get to know each other more intimately and have increased satisfaction with your relationship.

Ken says that the best thing about the whole decision-making process was that he really enjoyed talking with me more. We learned more about each other, and this made the relationship more enjoyable. In our first year of marriage, Ken and I experienced a wide separation in our thoughts on children. We established and followed the ground rules referenced in this book and were able to work on our differences, finally coming to a consensus that we both wanted children. Although we were never able to fulfill that wish, we think that the process that we went through to resolve our differences greatly contributed to our happiness today.

Of the process of resolving differences, Ken says, "Overall, when Donna finally was able to get through to me about how important a resolution was, everything clicked. The scary thing was that I was so dense on this issue. Thank God, Donna persisted. She tried everything she could think of, and then some. Talk about love! We communicated as a couple and continued to communicate until we reached a resolution that both of us could be in agreement. What about the next big conflict in our lives? I don't know what ours will be, but at least we now know that we can communicate better, and that we can resolve things and both be happy with the result."

On our tenth wedding anniversary, both of us expressed that time has passed so quickly we can hardly believe we've been married for ten years. I told Ken, "In a way it feels like we have been together forever and at the same time it feels like we fell in love yesterday."

If you and your partner are able to resolve your differences on children, you can apply those communication, problem-solving, and decision-making skills that you learn to other areas of your lives.

Many of the people in this book whose relationships survived the biggest issue they had to confront believe they have stronger marriages now. Brenda and Tom, having resolved their differences on children twice, are very happy and very much in love. They attribute their success to open communication and perseverance to work through their differences and decision-making as a team.

Julie and Tim identified early that their issue on children was related to Tim's own childhood experience. They worked on their differences, sharing equally in their desire for a favorable outcome. When they realized that Tim had some unresolved childhood issues, they sought out the help of a marriage and family therapist to assist him. Once those were resolved, the couple moved forward with their decision-making process on whether to start a family of their own. These were intimate moments that enriched their relationship and drew them closer. Today they enjoy a happy marriage and share their love with their two boys.

There is a closeness associated with resolving intimate problems and choices in life, such as the decision to have children. Discussions on this topic will usually unveil private emotions about your childhood, family values, core beliefs, and how you envision your future. These can be sensitive areas. But by sharing intimate details of your life with your partner, you can create a stronger sense of unity and trust. If the problem is resolved with honesty and not appeasement, the relationship has a greater chance of success and satisfaction. Remember too, that learning to compromise, at times, is also important to a successful relationship. Ensure that you and your partner trade off on compromises or one of you may feel resentment toward the other.

If you can resolve your differences on children, imagine how well you will be able to handle stressful situations in other aspects of your life (work, in-laws, social events, etc.). The benefit of having more open communications with your partner is a stronger union, which is the ultimate goal.

Studies support that a number of couples feel the success of their marriage and satisfaction level is due to the way they have resolved their differences through coactive communication and decision-making.[3] Every person is different, and there are differences in how men and women think. Eventually, you will both have to find a way to communicate—*really communicate*. When you do, the payoff can be enormous!

Chapter 13

Deciding to Have Children

C ongratulations! You and your partner have worked out your differences by coming to a healthy decision that works for both of you. Your lives will never be the same. Raising children can be one of the most rewarding yet challenging experiences a person will have during his or her lifetime. Most people are awestruck when they see their baby for the first time. They are consumed with total love and devotion for their child, along with the stunning realization that the creation of life is truly a miracle. Throughout each developmental stage—from newborn to toddler to preschool to grade school to adolescence—there can be an enormous amount of fulfillment and satisfaction in raising a child. There are also tremendous physical, financial, emotional, and sexual challenges that you and your partner may encounter when you have a child.

Often, couples feel that having a baby will give them a closer relationship. While it is true that over time, a child can bring a couple closer, what generally occurs is the opposite. Dr. Jay Belsky, coauthor of *The Transition to Parenthood* (Dell Publishing Company, 1995), studied 250 couples over a seven-year period. He found that, depending on the relationship and how well the couple adapts to parenthood, hidden differences might surface and push the couple apart. Those differences mainly concern values and the amount of work that is done by each partner. New parents also might find they have issues about money, changes in social life, and changes in their marriage (particularly a gap in the closeness they once enjoyed).

Dr. Belsky's study revealed that based on the couples' coping abilities to becoming new parents, there are four ways a marriage can change:

Severe Decliners: Twelve to 13 percent of all new parents experience a severe decline in marital satisfaction due to their vast differences in work and values. Differences can be so great they damage the relationship beyond repair.

Moderate Decliners: Thirty-eight percent of couples experience a moderate decline in marital happiness after they bring their baby home. They appear to be able to avoid any major upsets during their parenthood transition period, but still experience a drop in their satisfaction with each other.

No Change: Thirty percent of new parents were able to adjust to their differences enough to maintain the same marital satisfaction level they had pre-baby. However, this group did not experience greater closeness in their relationship after having a child.

Improvers: Surprisingly, 19 percent of couples actually fall more deeply in love after their child is born. Couples that experienced this improvement in their relationships were brought closer together by going through the process of acknowledging and overcoming their differences brought about by a new child.

Through his research, Dr. Belsky concluded that couples who were successful in transitioning into parenthood (those who experienced the same satisfaction level or greater marital satisfaction after the birth of their child) possessed the following six characteristics:

1. They worked together as a team and abandoned their individual needs and goals.
2. They settled their differences regarding the division of work with mutual satisfaction.
3. They found a way to deal with stress without placing additional stress on their marriage or their partner.
4. They fought constructively and continued to sustain a variety of common interests.
5. Even though their marriage may have improved after the baby, they were realistic to acknowledge that their marriage would never be the same as it was prior to the birth of their child.
6. They continued to nurture their relationship by communicating effectively and showing respect for each other.

New parents who do not have these six characteristics can review the list for helpful ways to improve their relationships.[1]

For those of you who feel arguments are damaging to your relationship, adoption of these six characteristics can aid in resolving conflict. Dr. Belsky also cites Dr. Gottman's findings that constructive arguing by married couples can improve a relationship because it allows each partner to share their point of view and feelings. Once each partner is aware of the other's position, the two can work on resolving differences.

Suppressing your thoughts can lead to frustration, misunderstandings, resentment, and possibly destructive behavior. Don't be shy about voicing your opinion on something that is near and dear to your heart, but be careful to express yourself in a constructive, nonthreatening manner.

It's important throughout a relationship to make certain that the same partner isn't doing all of the compromising in decisions. With a child, there are even more issues (between partners and between parents and child) to find compromises for. You and your partner will need to find a healthy balance for the amount of time you spend together, how often you have sex, how much time you have for yourself, and the amount of time you have for your career.

Most newborns sleep a lot but they need to be:

+ Fed every two to four hours
+ Burped
+ Changed frequently when their diapers are soiled
+ Soothed when they cry
+ Rocked back to sleep
+ Bathed

Activities become even more numerous and sometimes more difficult as the child grows, and then of course the child needs playtime as well. Even if you and your partner share in these responsibilities, this care can take a toll on your sleep patterns. Not enough sleep will interfere with your "fun time" in the bedroom, your career, and your social life. If you and your partner are considering the different aspects of having a child, be prepared to be sleep deprived for the first three to six months after you bring your baby home.

Along with a baby come a lot more expenses, and new parents must compromise on budgets. Baskets filled with diapers, bottles, powders, lotions, baby furniture, baby food, adorable clothes that they will only wear for one week before they outgrow them, toys, more toys, day care, babysitters, doctor's visits, college funding, and on and on. First-year expenses for your bundle of joy will average $13,000. So, don't be surprised if you feel your budget getting tighter. This is where you make compromises on the type of vacations you take, how often you go out or entertain, how much you put away for retirement, and how much you spend on yourselves for clothing and personal care. Actually, this is where you realize how selfless you really are.

Instead of a vacation in Hawaii, you may find yourself going to Disneyland . . . again! Instead of watching your favorite program, you may be entertained by Sponge Bob . . . for hours! Adult activities will be combined with children's activities. In fact, you'll be spending so much time with your child and other young children that you'll question if you will ever learn to talk like an adult again. Your choices in the food you prepare or dining establishments will change. Child-friendly food (corndogs, fries, chicken strips, peanut butter and jelly) will take on new importance when meal planning. Instead of a French restaurant, you may be going for fast food.

When you have a baby, you and your partner will need to work out your new roles and responsibilities and how you will share the load. You can alternate on the feeding, cleaning, schoolwork, and chauffeuring. (Just make sure that when it's your turn to drop your baby off at day care, you don't forget. Even though your baby is as cute as a button, he won't be welcome at your manager's staff meeting.) Sharing in your baby's care will help reduce the stress on both you and your partner, increase the bond you have with your child, and potentially increase your relationship satisfaction.

Quiet time for you and your spouse will seem to be a thing of the past. Any quiet time from here until your child moves out will be cherished and will most likely occur during your child's naptime or when he or she is at a sleepover. Sex may also be a thing of the past, or at least the frequency of sex will not be the same after a baby. This is mainly due to sleep deprivation and exhaustion.

Finding time together as a couple is more challenging after a baby. Make it a priority to find time to talk with each other for at least fifteen minutes a day. Talk about how your day went and really focus on each other. You'll be surprised at how important the simple things in life are. Make time to go out to dinner, a movie, or even for a walk, just the two of you, at least once a week, and go somewhere overnight every couple of months. At first, you may want to call the babysitter every fifteen minutes when you are apart from your child, but eventually you'll adjust and enjoy the special time that you and your partner have together.

Finding time alone as an individual will also be important. All of us need time to unwind, collect our thoughts, and be at peace with ourselves. Taking a break, time out just for you, can be rejuvenating. It can also make you a more pleasant person to be around. When either you or your partner needs time alone, ask the other for support and respect. Each of you can help by attending to the needs of the baby while the other takes a break.

Having a baby can bring incredible opportunities and joy. Many couples experience a sense of endearing pride and unconditional love for their child—at least until the "terrible twos" hit. For some couples, having a baby is their greatest achievement in life. For them, nothing else compares. They have the opportunity to become a father, a mom, a role model, a teacher, a mentor, a protector. They have the ability to make a difference in someone's life. For people who long to be parents, these roles can be exceptionally fulfilling. Following are some thoughts from couples in this book who had children and who felt it was an amazing experience for the entire family.

Bill and Gail, Chapter 8

Bill: "Watching something come to life that you've created is the most beautiful and rewarding experience I have ever had. I was in the delivery room for both my sons. And I'll admit it, I cried with both my boys. It's an amazing thing.

"What's also incredible to see are the continuous changes our boys have gone through. The growth spurts, the whole developmental process, and their ability to learn so quickly. It's amazing. I can't tell you how much our boys have changed since they were first born. In fact, after the birth of our first son, we went out and purchased a camcorder."

Gail: "We wanted to put everything on film because we didn't want to miss out on anything. We never had a need for a camcorder before, and now we don't know what we'd do without one. We have a whole library filled with videos of our boys growing up. Some nights when the boys are asleep we'll sit here and reminisce while watching home videos of our kids."

Bill and Gail both feel they are having the time of their lives with the boys and that they can't imagine life without their kids.

Bill and Gail's attention is often focused on their children and not on each other. The distance is something that happens when people have children; less attention is given to each other. Bill and Gail have a strong marriage and are happy with each other and their family.

Julie and Tim, Chapters 2, 4, 11, 12

For Julie, everything about being a mother is enjoyable. She says that before she had children she felt unbalanced, like something was missing, and she didn't know what that something was. Now she feels complete. She says that her life is much more satisfying with children than before.

Tim says that after they had children their circle of friends changed, but it didn't matter. Most couples feel they automatically have something in common with anyone who has children. Vacations also changed. They now do more camping and Club Med packages for families. Julie has been fortunate enough to be home to raise their children and she will continue to stay home as long as she can. Julie feels that motherhood has been a full-time, and rewarding, job for her. Julie and Tim have adjusted to their life-style changes and accepted their new roles as parents. They have formed a content and happy family.

Brenda and Tom, Chapters 1, 6, 12

Brenda: "The rewards about being a parent are that you have this unique love for your child—more than loving yourself, it's a different love than what you have for your husband, for your parents, and your siblings. Every day is filled with hugs and kisses, and we all say 'I love you' several times a day. Sometimes, you have to operate in survival mode for the day. You do what needs to be done and what doesn't need to be done really isn't important. You have a different perspective."

Tom: "I cherish our children's play time and don't worry about the mess. The other day I was relaxing on the couch while Brenda was breast-feeding our youngest. Our two daughters ages four and six were putting on a play for us. They went into their bedroom and pulled clothes out of their drawers. When they came out, they had underwear on their heads and socks on their hands. Those are incredible moments."

Brenda and Tom adore their children and are enjoying every moment of being a parent.

These couples have similarities that contribute to the success of their relationship. They take time out to talk with each other. They also make it a priority to go out on a date at least once a month. They seem to know the importance of communication in sustaining their relationship. Their lives aren't always filled with bliss, though. When they encounter issues over differences, they pull together as a team and resolve the conflict in the same manner they did when deciding to have children. They have learned the importance of compromise, have accepted the changes in their lives, and have grown as individuals while participating in the most challenging and satisfying job they will ever have—being a parent.

Your experience in resolving your differences about having children should give you the foundation of how you can work through future situations. Now that you have decided to have a child, recognize that your lives will never be the same, keep your communication open, work together as a team, and resolve issues in a constructive manner that has a mutually satisfying outcome. If you follow these guidelines, you can experience a more satisfying relationship after the birth of your child.

Chapter 14

Living Child-Free

After much discussion and soul-searching, you and your partner have decided to live child-free. The two of you have gone through your decision-making process and have concluded that you thoroughly enjoy your relationship as it is and do not want to complicate it with children. Or, you may no longer wish to pursue having children for medical or psychological reasons.

Depending on how you came to your consensus (compromise, conviction, agreement, or infertility), you may experience emotional backlashes that will need to be acknowledged. Those emotions can include grief, anger, resentment, loss, acceptance, and perhaps even regret later on in your relationship. Be careful not to suppress your emotions, or they can jeopardize your relationship.

Some couples are absolutely content without having children. They have freedom to be spontaneous and have uninterrupted evenings, the ability to spend and invest their money as they see fit, freedom to travel, and they have more time to devote to each other and their careers. For them, a child would be an obstacle preventing them from obtaining their dreams.

Some women regret their decision to postpone motherhood or to remain child-free because if they decide they do want children, it is often too late and they are infertile. As a result, many of these women feel resentment toward their partner. Some express their resentment openly, while others suppress their emotions for years, stewing until they feel as if they will explode.

Dawn, now in her early fifties, is an example of someone who did not have children and resents her husband for it. At first she thought, "My husband kept postponing children until it was too late for us to have any at all. I still resent him for that!" She loves her husband dearly and has been with him for thirty years. Dawn never envisioned her life without children and even though she agreed to postpone children, she still blames her husband. She said she never would have agreed to postpone children if she knew she wouldn't be able to have children later in her life.

Dawn was quick to support her position, placing blame elsewhere and not taking any personal responsibility in the decision to postpone the start of a family. This was a classic display of resentment. The word *resent* means to feel strongly about something. *Re* means to repeat or to go back. So, resentment could be defined as meaning to re-feel or to feel again. Many therapists believe the reason that some people keep feeling something over and over again is that they haven't learned or haven't grown from the experience. This is mainly because they have not confronted the effects of their participation in the decision-making or handled their feelings appropriately for their actions in the situation.

In Dawn's circumstance, she believed her husband was responsible for their childless lifestyle. Dawn felt he discounted her need to have a child, and she resented it. If Dawn examined their past though, she would realize she also agreed to postpone the start of a family. She did not express her expectations or hopes of having a child "later on," and her husband assumed that she completely agreed with him. They are good candidates for therapy so that Dawn and her husband can understand that she gave him the power to decide for her, and he made an assumption that was not clarified. Dawn needs help to accept that she was involved in the decision, and she needs to express and resolve her feelings of resentment. Her husband needs to learn that making assumptions in major decisions is ineffective, at the very least, and may be destructive in the worst circumstances. Both partners must be involved in the reconciliation and the healing of their wounds for both to move forward in their lives.

Remember Cathy from Chapter 6, page 76, who wanted more children even though she already had two? Her husband Ernie said, "No more kids!" and because he didn't want to get a vasectomy, he convinced her to get a tubal ligation. She succumbed to his wishes even though she didn't want to go through with the operation. Later she divorced Ernie and married a man who wanted to have children with her. Unfortunately, Cathy's tubal ligation procedure removed too much of her fallopian tubes for reconnection. Cathy spent years dealing with her regret about her operation and blamed herself for her unwanted sterility. When Cathy finally acknowledged that she too was responsible for her actions, agreeing to the operation, she was able to stop blaming herself, accept her situation, and feel at peace with herself and her life.

Accepting Your Decision

Many women who have agreed not to have children, and then change their minds but still remain childless, will be overcome by a sense of loss. This is also true for women who are childless due to infertility. Women who vacillated on their decision about children may not be completely convinced once they decide to be child-free. But, because of love for and commitment to their partner, they don't want to give up the relationship. In these situations, there is a deep grief linked to the inability to have children. Often women will mourn as if someone has died, and this can manifest itself through a wave of emotions including sadness, anger, guilt, fear, confusion, numbness, and even depression.

During this grieving period, many women experience physical and mental changes such as loss of appetite, inability to concentrate, and fatigue. If you feel this way, you need to work through the emotions associated with loss. The biggest step is to acknowledge your responsibility in the decision to be child-free and openly accept the lifestyle choice. With almost 20 percent of the United States population remaining childless, the acceptance of childless couples is growing along with the trend.[1]

It really is okay to choose to be child-free. Many women and men are successful without having children in their lives. The same is true for women who are childless due to infertility. They need to accept their fate. Although the two circumstances seem different, they are similar. In both situations, the women most likely will not conceive a child and may mourn for the baby and family they will never have. Acceptance is a huge element in the healing process.

Staying physically active, even if it's just walking, and keeping socially active will help you get through this emotionally trying time. This grieving process takes time. When Ken and I were in the middle of our discussions about having a child, a therapist told me that if I supported my husband's desire to not have children, it could take me three to four years to actually accept a child-free lifestyle. During your healing process, be patient and treat yourself well. Remind yourself of past accomplishments and focus on your goals. Realize that your life can be fulfilling without children. Appreciate your partner, value your relationship, and envision a rewarding future. If you feel you need assistance, seek out a therapist who is trained in grief counseling. There are many therapists who are trained in this area of counseling and who will be able to help you get through the grieving process.

Your partner needs to understand your sacrifice and to be supportive. He will need to show patience, compassion, understanding, and appreciation for your level of commitment to the relationship. When you are grieving, you need to verbalize what you want him to say or do. Do you want to be alone for twenty minutes every day? Do you want him to sit beside you and hold your hand? Do you need him only to listen to you, to not give advice, suggestions, etc.? Tell him explicitly what will be the most helpful for you. He can't read your mind and he likely won't express his feelings of loss in the same way you will. Tell him, respectfully, what he can do to help you through this time.

Birth Control in a Child-free Life

If you decide to remain childless and need to pursue birth control, you have temporary and permanent options. Temporary birth control, such as the Pill, shots, patches, condoms, and IUDs, allow freedom of choice if you change your mind. A vasectomy or tubal ligation is considered a permanent form of birth control. The procedure for reversing a vasectomy or tubal ligation can be costly and success rates are not guaranteed. If you are still not absolutely sure about whether to have children, choose a temporary form of birth control. Chapter 9 discussed your options and potential drawbacks for temporary versus permanent birth control.

Is there any chance that either you or your partner will change your minds about remaining child-free? Absolutely. Your decision not to have children may change as you mature. After all, the desire to have children is a natural biological instinct. Our bodies were designed to procreate. When that maternal impulse kicks in, many women are unable to resist the urge to conceive.

You might even end up wanting to change partners because your relationship has gone as far as it could. The next relationship may be with a partner who wants a family as much as you do.

For those who are certain about their decision not to reproduce, a tubal ligation or a vasectomy can provide peace of mind. Taking action before you reach thirty to permanently strip yourself of your fertility may have severe emotional consequences that you will have to deal with for years to come. An article on poststerilization regret, by Hillis SD et al., reveals that around 20 percent of women who underwent a tubal liga-tion before or at age thirty regretted their decision fourteen years later.[2] When you are considering your options, keep in mind that permanent birth control is a huge decision that can dramatically affect your life.

Though you decided not to have children, you may still feel as if you need an outlet for nurturing. If you find that having a pet is not enough, look into volunteer programs where you can help children. In volunteer-ing, you're not only helping yourself, but you're helping others too. Schools, churches, libraries, and organizations are always looking for volunteers to assist them with their programs for children. Local newspapers usu-ally list organizations and groups that meet regularly or sponsor projects needing volunteers. You can also go to your local city council or volunteer bureau to learn more about how to get involved.

You should also look for ways to nurture yourself. Focus on the positives and not the negatives, be patient, and treat yourself with care. Observe your personal improvements, regardless of how small, and allow yourself to feel appreciation for success. Ask your friends for their sup-port—most of them will want to help you overcome your challenges. And learn to love yourself.

If you find that you need additional support to help you with your child-free lifestyle, seek out and make friends with other childless cou-ples. Join an organization or two that doesn't include or focus on children. Find a support group in your area. (See the Appendix section on page 185 for books and Web sites.)

Living child-free has its advantages. You have more time to spend together as a couple, more spontaneity than people with children have, and more freedom with your time. Count your blessings and accentuate what you have!

Chapter 15

Treating Infertility

You've decided to have children, and you and your partner have been having unprotected sex for a little over six months. He's been smiling much more and you've become very conscious of your fertility calendar, but nothing has happened. You begin having concerns. *Am I able to get pregnant at my age? What if I have a fertility problem?*

In today's era of older women having babies, more women feel they too can achieve pregnancy at a later age. Many women do not take into consideration the emotional, physical, and financial costs associated with having a baby at an older age. According to the American Infertility Association, infertility affects more than 15 percent of couples living in the United States who are trying to conceive.[1]

So, how old is too old, and when does the clock stop ticking? Fertility studies on women have found that peak fertility usually occurs when a woman is in her twenties and begins to decline slowly when she reaches her late twenties.[2] After age thirty-five, this decline becomes more rapid

until menopause. Most experts will agree that the "critical age" for women trying to bear children is thirty-five. Women are born with all the eggs they will ever have during their lifetime; as they age, so do their eggs.[3] Throughout their lives, women's eggs are affected by everything they are exposed to—x-rays, medication, chemicals, etc.—and as a result, some eggs will have damaged chromosomes. The older you get, the greater the chance for birth defects.

The most common birth defects in children borne by women over thirty-five are Down's syndrome and spina bifida.[4] Nearly all birth defects are related to chromosomal disorders, and about half of these types of pregnancies will result in miscarriages, with most occurring in the first few weeks of pregnancy.

An amniocentesis procedure is available to test the amniotic fluid for chromosomal abnormalities, but this test is not performed until the tenth or eleventh week of pregnancy. If chromosomal damage is detected, serious decisions need to be made about whether to terminate the pregnancy. No one can say exactly what she would do until she is faced with such a dilemma.

Also, the older you are when you get pregnant, the more susceptible you are to dangerous conditions such as high blood pressure, pre-eclampsia, toxemia, and gestational diabetes, which is usually diagnosed in the third trimester. None of these are long-term conditions (they usually end after delivery), but some can be life threatening to both mother and baby if left untreated.

Conceiving naturally in your forties is possible, but with much more difficulty and with more health risks to you and the child. Doctors recommend taking folic acid to help reduce the risk of birth defects, but there is no guarantee that both mother and baby will have an easy time.[5] Celebrity pregnancies where the mom-to-be is in her forties make great news stories, but understand that these are typically achieved via in vitro fertilization (IVF) and sometimes also with egg donation.

How Do You Know If You Have a Fertility Problem?

Doctors have defined infertility for women under thirty-five as the inability to conceive after one year of unprotected active sex.[6] For women thirty-five and older, the timeline for infertility is after six months of active unprotected sex. Infertility can also include the inability to complete a pregnancy to full-term (having a miscarriage), as well as other physical problems such as tubal blockage (you), low sperm count (him), lack of ovulation (you), etc. Basically, if you fall into any of these categories, and you want children, or think that you might want children in the future, you and your partner should seek medical assistance to verify your fertility or infertility.

If you feel you may have an infertility issue, your family doctor or obstetrician/gynecologist is the best resource to start asking questions. He or she can refer you to specialists if needed. Prior to sending you to a specialist though, your doctor may conduct some preliminary fertility tests to identify the problem. Depending on your situation, your doctor may choose to refer you directly to an infertility specialist, normally called a reproductive endocrinologist (RE).

Preliminary Fertility Tests

Fertility is not just about you being able to get pregnant—it takes two to tango, remember! Thirty-five percent of fertility issues for couples are linked to problems in the woman, 35 percent to the man; 20 percent are linked to problems with both partners; and the remaining 10 percent are undetermined.[7] When doctors are looking for the infertility problem, you both need to be examined. That is, unless one of you already has prior medical knowledge of a specific problem that may be causing your infertility. Don't make the assumption that it's just your body getting older, or that you keep forgetting to stand on your head after intercourse to improve your chances (an old wives' tale). There is an equal chance that he may be the infertile one.

When you visit the doctor or clinic, they will be looking for some specific indicators. Based on your problem and medical history, your doctor may wish to perform additional tests.

For Women:

+ A physical examination.
+ Study of your menstrual cycles. You may want to track your menstrual cycles for as many of the previous months as possible and give these to your doctor. Charting your basal body temps (using a digital thermometer, which you can get at most drugstores) for the same time frame will also provide the doctor with more valuable information, as will the results of any home ovulation predictor tests that you have.
+ Blood tests to measure hormone levels for any imbalances. Doctors are most interested in measuring your follicle-stimulating hormone (FSH) to determine whether your body is producing enough hormones to grow and develop a mature egg. The blood test will also measure your luteinizing hormone (LH) to see if your body is producing enough of that hormone to release an egg into your uterus.[8]
+ A hysterosalpingogram (HSG) test. With this exam, a dye is injected through the cervix into the uterus and fallopian tubes. This test can be slightly uncomfortable and can cause some cramping. An x-ray then reveals the shape of the uterus and can detect any abnormalities including blockages in the fallopian tubes.[9]
+ Ovulation scan. This is an ultrasound procedure used for checking the thickness of the lining of the uterus (the endometrial lining) during an LH surge. A thin lining indicates inadequate hormone production or can mean that the body isn't responding to the level of hormones being produced. This test is also used for observing ovulation and can assist in identifying any reproductive abnormalities. It is very useful in detecting ovarian cysts, small tumors, and any fibroid growth, which can indicate endometriosis

(endometrial tissue that grows outside the uterine area).[10]

+ Postcoital test. The postcoital examination determines if you have "fertile" mucus. During an LH surge, the vaginal mucus is clear and very flexible.[11]

+ Subsequent visits will be scheduled to review your tests and for any additional tests that the doctor may feel are necessary.

For Men:

+ Examination of medical history and medical records. The doctor is looking for any illnesses or diseases that could affect sperm such as mumps, diabetes, fevers, cancer, or sexually transmitted diseases.[12] The doctor will also ask about sexually transmitted diseases and sexual history. Some of these questions may be embarrassing, but they are necessary to determine if there is a problem.

+ Physical examination. A physical evaluation will include an examination of his testes/scrotum for any abnormalities such as varicoceles (varicose veins).

+ Semen sample. The doctor will request a semen sample. The sample should be obtained after two days of abstention (tell him you'll make it up to him later) and most likely will need to be collected on site (labs will have magazines). Sometimes, special arrangements can be made to collect the sample outside of the lab. Do not use off-the-shelf condoms for the sample because the spermicides present will kill any live sperm. If a condom is needed, a doctor can provide a special condom specifically for sperm collection.

+ Additional semen tests may be necessary. Remember that the sperm donated will reflect what went on in his life eight to ten weeks ago. If he partied too hard then, it may affect his test results.

+ A follow-up visit will be scheduled to discuss the results and to schedule any additional testing needed.

The tests are minimally invasive, but may be a little embarrassing, especially to your partner. The doctor can and should explain each test to you, and sometimes may ask one or both of you to complete additional testing.

Once these preliminary examinations are completed, you will have a better idea of what your chances are to conceive a child. If the doctor finds that you or your partner has infertility issues, today's technology now offers a number of fertility treatments that you can undergo to improve your chances of getting pregnant.

Where You Go from There

Your insurance may cover some of the preliminary tests, but most insurance providers will not cover any of the expenses for fertility procedures. If your situation requires "assistance" to get pregnant, your doctor will advise you of what your best options are, given your health, age, financial capability, and how you feel about fertility treatments.

Bear in mind that this area of medicine is changing rapidly as new techniques are developed and approved. Again, your infertility specialist will consult with you on what technique is best given your age, health, financial resources, and willingness to let science help nature.

Everything Is Okay

Keep trying. You now know that it's likely just a matter of time and luck before you conceive. If you are still unsure of whether you want a child, or if you will want children sometime in the future, you will need to take precautions (birth control of some sort). Be happy—you are a fertile couple!

You Are Both Fertile, But . . .

You now know that some assistance will be needed because of issues with either you or your partner. It may seem disappointing, but you now know what was going on. Depending on the diagnosis, you will have several options. First, your doctor will ask you and your partner about cleaning up your lifestyles. Fertility difficulties can be a result of the things you put into your bodies. Recreational drugs, drinking to excess, smoking, and exposure to certain chemicals can affect your ability to conceive a healthy child. Following are some of the procedures and drugs that may be administered to either you or your partner. The treatments are listed from the simplest and least expensive to the most complex. Your doctor will discuss side effects, and the fact that women who undergo hormone treatments, including Clomiphene and Pergonal injections, are at a higher risk for getting uterine, ovarian, and cervical cancer.

Clomiphene (for You)

Many doctors like to start their patients out with Clomiphene Citrate (Clomid, Serophene). It's a synthetic hormone that basically revs up a woman's reproductive system. Clomiphene does this by stimulating the hypothalamus in the brain to release more gonadotropin hormones (GnRH). When it does, the pituitary responds by releasing more LH and FSH. When that happens, the ovary is stimulated to produce a mature egg. Clomiphene is also used to help women who have a luteal phase defect (LPD). With this problem, a woman begins the ovulation process, but something disrupts it, causing the level of progesterone to drop. (Progesterone is the hormone that prepares the uterine lining for implantation of a fertilized egg.) If the level of progesterone drops while a fertilized egg is in the uterus, successful implantation might be prohibited. If implantation does occur, this drop can cause a woman to begin her period and end the pregnancy. When a woman takes Clomiphene, her body produces more LH and FSH hormones and her ovaries can manufacture progesterone throughout the right time frame; if the egg becomes fertilized, she has more chance of retaining the pregnancy. Side effects, in general, include hot flashes, premenstrual-type symptoms, enlargement of the ovaries, and a slight increase for having twins.[13] This is the most inexpensive fertility treatment, around $50 a cycle plus doctor's visits.

Pergonal (for You)

Pergonal injections are the hormone treatments that accompany artificial insemination (AI) and are also used for in vitro fertilization (IVF). In brief, Pergonal causes multiple eggs to be released during ovulation. Side effects include the possibility of enlarged ovaries, pelvic discomfort, mood swings, multiple pregnancies, and cyst development. Be prepared that once you commit to Pergonal treatments, your life will be controlled by your menstrual cycle and numerous office visits.[14] Pergonal injections are administered (often by your partner at home) according to your cycle. In addition to Pergonal injections, you will most likely need to take estrogen tablets to help elevate your estrogen level. There is also an egg drop injection, referred to as human chorionic gonadotropin (hCG), that you will need to administer. It's similar to luteinizing hormone and stimulates the eggs to be released from the follicles (ovulation). Once ovulation occurs, your body is prepared for artificial insemination.[15] Pergonal is a natural product (made by purifying the gonadotropin hormones in the urine of menopausal woman) and can be expensive.

Artificial Insemination (AI) (for Both of You)

If he has some sperm deficiencies, AI is likely your first option. Here your partner will be asked to provide a sperm sample, which is then "washed" to concentrate the sperm and remove any abnormal sperm and toxic substances.[16] You will likely be asked to take fertility drugs to improve your chances of conception. Costs for this procedure along with the fertility drugs are relatively inexpensive, around $2,000–$3,000 per attempt.

In Vitro Fertilization (IVF) (for Both of You)

IVF, increasing in popularity in the United States, combines shots of Clomiphene and Pergonal with artificial insemination, except that in IVF, the eggs are "harvested" from you and inseminated outside your body.[17] The fertilized eggs are then placed back into your uterus to grow. Multiple births are a distinct possibility here. Success rates vary with your age, but 33 percent success per cycle (attempt) is about average.[18] After age thirty-five, there is a steep decline in success rates, and your doctor may suggest using donor eggs to improve your chances. Multiple attempts are common for couples that choose IVF. Each cycle's cost will range from $12,000 to $18,000—IVF is not cheap.[19]

One or Both of You Have Fertility Issues

Knowledge is a powerful thing, and you now have an idea of what is necessary to conceive. Perhaps you knew, going into this, that your diagnosis would be along these lines because he has had a vasectomy or you had a tubal ligation. You both still have options for pregnancy.

Vasovasostomy

In most cases of vasovasostomies, rule number one is to make sure that the woman is fertile or sterile. Then your doctor should help you understand difficulties likely to occur if you follow this path. When Ken and I went through this, I assumed that I would not have a problem in getting pregnant, despite my age. Had we known the problems we would encounter, we might have made another decision. That said, your partner might opt to undergo a reverse vasectomy. Microsurgery is up to 90 percent successful, with the success rate decreasing if the reversal is attempted ten or more years after the initial surgery.[20] Costs range from $4,000 to $20,000 depending on the procedure and hospitalization.[21] (For recovery tips, see the advice on pages 102 and 103 in Chapter 8.)

Sperm Retrieval

In this procedure, the doctor will "harvest" the sperm directly from the testis or epididymis and proceed with implantation through IVF techniques.[22] Success rates will be similar to IVF, and multiple attempts may be necessary. Costs for this procedure, including the IVF portion, will be between $20,000 and $25,000 per attempt. If you have fertility issues of your own, sperm retrieval is often recommended over a vasovasostomy for financial reasons.

Tubal Ligation Reversal

If your tubes have been tied, it is possible to get the procedure reversed. Your tubes will be reconnected via microsurgery. Success rates are very good at about 85 percent. The cost will be between $10,000 and $18,000, depending on your situation and whether the procedure is done in a hospital stay or on an outpatient basis.[23]

Sperm Donation

If he is infertile, sperm donation is a possibility for you.[24] Your doctor can refer you to a sperm bank where frozen samples are available for your selection. You will have some knowledge of the donor's physical traits and characteristics, but you will never know his name. Costs for the sperm will be about $250, plus you will need to undergo the insemination procedure described in sperm retrieval. You can also choose to obtain sperm from a friend.

Egg Donation

As in sperm donation, you can choose an egg based on the general traits of the donor.[25] The egg is implanted via IVF. Costs can be about $9,000 but may be included in a "package" deal with the clinic's IVF program.[26] Success rates with fresh donor eggs versus frozen donor eggs are significantly better according to a report issued by the U.S. Department of Health and Human Services.

Surrogates

If you are capable of producing eggs but you may have difficulty carrying the baby to term, surrogacy may be an option.[27] Costs would include the IVF procedure plus any fees given to the surrogate and both of your attorneys.

What You Can Expect

There may be several variations for each of the outlined procedures. Be certain that you understand exactly what will be required of both you and your partner, what will be performed, when each procedure needs to be done to be most effective, how expensive your treatments will be, and the doctor's best "guesstimate" of your success rates for conception and a full-term baby. Success rates from clinics depend on many issues, including the clinic's willingness to take candidates with low probability situations. Ask lots of questions.

Make sure that you know what your emotional and financial thresholds will be when you begin exploring infertility options. Many couples become obsessed about succeeding in their quest to have a baby. They get caught up in trying one treatment after another until they succeed, or until they have depleted their financial resources, or they can no longer continue with treatments emotionally or physically. Infertility treatments can be very rewarding for those who succeed, but they can also be very demanding as your body reacts to hormonal changes and the emotional letdowns that accompany multiple attempts and failures.

Your doctor will most likely suggest trying the least invasive (and least expensive) procedures first. Make sure you and your partner agree on how far you are willing to go based on your financial ability, your ethical beliefs, and your emotional ability to accept cycle failures (33 percent means two of three attempts fail in healthy women) especially when your fertility hormones may be affecting you.

You may want to join a support group or organization such as RESOLVE. RESOLVE is an excellent source of infertility information and helps women deal with decision-making, their feelings, and the medical and emotional impacts that go along with infertility.

When Ken and I were faced with fertility issues, we agreed to use artificial insemination with Ken's sperm. I knew I faced emotional highs and lows with the bimonthly Pergonal injections. We pushed the science of conception as far as we were comfortable and chose not to try donor eggs and IVF. We were willing to help nature a little but not too much. After each failure of our four AI attempts, I became more despondent until I decided no more. After a year of recovery, Ken and I became interested in adoption as an alternative.

Thirty-five-year-old Toni didn't know she had a fertility problem when her husband, Phil, underwent a vasovasostomy. After six months of not getting pregnant, Toni decided to see a fertility specialist and was told her tubes were blocked. She underwent an operation to correct the problem and became pregnant the following month. Toni and Phil have two beautiful boys spaced two years apart.

It took two long years of treatments at an infertility clinic before Rachael finally got pregnant and had a daughter. Of the treatment she says, "You don't realize it, but you get so caught up in the process. You go through the first treatment and find yourself moving onto the next, and then the next one after that." Rachael adores her little girl, but because of the infertility treatment roller coaster, she and her husband will not try for a second child.

If you decide to supplement nature with fertility treatments, here's a five-step recommendation for men from my husband:

1. Find a good doctor with whom you're comfortable. The doctor is going to ask you all kinds of intimate questions. Be prepared for that.
2. Find out all of your options. What can happen? What are the side effects? What are the chances? How much is it going to cost? Understand completely what you are about to undertake.
3. If sperm samples are to be collected, you are about to lose any sense of dignity that you once had. Sperm donation is your partner's revenge for all those years of stirrups and Pap smears.
4. If your partner is on fertility drugs, *do not* make any jokes about her weight. Better yet, don't make any jokes at all. Trust me on this one.
5. Be supportive. Remember why you're doing this.

Chapter 16

Adoption as an Option

Many people look into adoption when they realize they cannot produce a biological child of their own. In most cases, the struggle with infertility has left them with a severe sense of loss. This can be a heartbreaking and sometimes spirit-breaking time. Mourning the fact of never being able to experience pregnancy or child-birth may take years to overcome. Even with infertility, many women and their partners still hope to have a family, and adoption is one way to make their dream become a reality.

Deciding to adopt and then carrying it out is not easier, and in fact is often more complicated than making the decision to have a biological baby. There is a complete paradigm shift involved with adoption. The biggest shift is that of acceptance. You and your partner must accept that:

- You will not have a biological child of your own.
- You need to have enough love in your heart to raise someone else's child as if he or she were your own.

+ The adoption process is lengthy.
+ You need to relate to the needs and emotions of the birth mother and how difficult this must be for her.
+ The birth mother is giving you a precious gift and entrusting her child to you.
+ You are going to be a parent and will be responsible for the welfare of the child you adopt.

Many new questions arise with the premise of adoption, and both you and your partner will need to do some serious soul-searching. Ask yourselves the following questions:

+ Are you emotionally ready?
+ Do you still have hope that someday you'll get pregnant?
+ Does one of you want to adopt more than the other?
+ Is it important that the child look like you and your partner?
+ Are you able to accept, love, and raise someone else's child as if he or she were your own?
+ What if the baby has a disability?
+ What if the disability isn't detected until the child is older?

Hundreds of thousands of children are in need of adoption every year. If you're thinking of adopting, you'll want to educate yourself as much as possible on the subject to ensure that you are doing the right thing for you, your relationship, and the child. You and your partner need to determine if adoption is right for you after the time and effort you spent trying to have your own biological child.

You both may want to have a child, you have the means to raise a child in an atmosphere that will provide a nurturing environment, and you have the ability to handle the challenges that come with having and raising a child. Still, you need to consider many factors before you decide to go through with it. First, this child will not be connected to you biologically nor will he have been inside your womb (as with some IVF possibilities). If this reality is a concern for either you or your partner, do not consider the adoption process until you can resolve this issue. Would you love this child as you would your biological child? If you have the slightest doubt (or even if you don't doubt it at all), do some homework. Talk to an organization that can help educate you on the adoption process and various services, talk to your church leader, or better yet, talk to an adoptive parent. By talking to experienced people about adoption, you can hear their stories and ask questions about the doubts they may have had as they pondered this important decision. You may find out that you're on par with others in your reservations. But, if you cannot resolve your doubts successfully . . . stop!

Second, once you've decided that you are ready to adopt, you'll want to prepare yourself for what to expect. You will undergo a regulated evaluation conducted by a state agency. They will determine if you will be acceptable parents. Each state has its own criteria for evaluating adoptive parents. At a minimum, they look for any criminal history, psychological problems, job stability, and the ability to provide a suitable home for the child. Fingerprints are taken, a background check is performed, and at least one home visit is scheduled to interview and assess your residence. You will be asked a number of questions, usually beginning with why you want to adopt. Some states may also require you to take a parenting class and a first-aid class (which you should do even if it's not required). They are not looking for perfect people living in a mansion; just be yourselves, be open, and ask them questions along the way. If you pass, the agency will then make a recommendation and approve you for adoption.

The law gives adoption agencies leeway in determining the demographics of who can be a parent.[1] Married couples, singles, people over forty or under forty, gay people, or disabled people can all legally adopt in the United States. You are also allowed to have flaws; i.e., you don't have to be perfect. However, you will find that many adoption agencies may have incorporated their own adoption criteria into the services they provide. Agencies connected with religious organizations may require that both you and your partner are members of their faith and promise to raise the child in that faith. Other agencies may require that prospective parents be under the age of forty. If you choose to use an agency, consider shopping around to find the agency that will allow for any special needs that you may have.

Once you have found an agency and passed any criteria posed by the state and the agency, you will need to select which adoption process you want—there are many. Planned Parenthood, local adoption agencies, religious organizations, or adoption education organizations, such as RESOLVE, are also excellent places to begin the selection of the adoption process that is right for you. RESOLVE hosts an all-day seminar, usually held on a Saturday, once or twice a year. These seminars are an excellent way to learn about the different types of adoption options. In some locations, RESOLVE also offers once-a-month meetings on adoption.

Domestic Private Agency Adoption

The agency will help you through the process of scheduling your home study, finding a birth mother in the United States (although often only in your state), covering the birth mother's expenses, including delivery, and coordinating the legal documentation as you progress through the process. They usually offer counseling services, birth mother letter assistance, and postadoption guidance. Agencies also usually offer open or closed adoption options. In most cases, with an open adoption, you will have contact with the birth mother prior to and after the baby's birth. Initially, this may seem awkward, but knowing the birth mother can become very beneficial to all involved. With a closed adoption, there is no contact between the birth mother and the adoptive parents and the baby's birth records are sealed.

Domestic private agency adoption costs range from $8,000 to $30,000 and up.[2] Variation in price depends on the services provided, any complications during the birth, and if you qualify for a fee reduction due to income. The advantage with this type of adoption is that experienced, caring people will assist you with whatever difficulties or questions you may encounter. The disadvantage is that private agencies may have a variety of restrictions on whom they assist with adoption.

Domestic Independent Adoption

Independent adoption is usually arranged through an attorney who assists you in locating a birth mother or child in the United States. The attorney usually helps you locate a child or birth mother through newspaper ads, and then arranges payment for expenses incurred by the birth mother, and advises you on any legal issues proposed during the process. The attorney should handle all monies during the process and instruct you not to send money directly to the birth mother. Since this process can be more susceptible to scams, the attorney should obtain medical proof of pregnancy and talk to the birth mother's doctor prior to paying her any expense money.

Expenses for domestic independent adoption can range from $8,000 to $30,000 and up.[3] Advertising expenses can vary widely depending on the newspaper (big cities, big costs) and the length of time the ad runs. The big advantage of this type of adoption is that the attorney represents you. You won't be dealing with an agency that may reject you due to age, marital status, etc., and the time period needed to find a baby can be shorter than going through an agency. However, in the event that the birth mother changes her mind, you will not be reimbursed for any medical expenses paid. Also, the advertising process is restricted in some states and counseling assistance is not provided.

Domestic Public Agency Adoptions

These adoptions are typically for children with special needs. Many of these children have been taken by Child Service Agencies and include a variety of ages from infants to toddlers to teenagers. The child may be perfectly healthy, or he or she may have special medical or counseling needs. These children can be the most difficult to place with adoptive families because they tend to have the most needs, but they can also offer heart-warming rewards to patient adoptive families.

Because of the special needs of many of these children, most states heavily subsidize the adoption expenses.[4] This means you will receive financial assistance to care for your adopted special-needs child. Depending on the child's requirements, state financial support may continue for the child's expenses after the adoption. The processing time to adopt a child through a public agency can be relatively short because, unfortunately, there always seem to be children available. You will likely need to have more patience, to spend more time, and to give more love to raise a child adopted through a public agency. Make sure that you are able to handle any special needs that the child may have before you commit. If you adopt a special-needs child and, then, decide you cannot cope with the extra responsibilities required to care for this child, her self-esteem and emotional stability may be severely damaged.

International Adoption

International adoption is done through an agency that specializes in arranging adoptions of children born in other countries. In addition to having to meet the requirements of your state, you may also face additional requirements from the child's home country. The agency should arrange for all adoptive and immigration paperwork, should locate the child, and should provide some counseling services. Depending on the country and the shelter where the child resides, you may get complete health records for the child and his parents, or you may get nothing. The agency will also help you make arrangements to travel to the country to pick up the child. Most likely, the agency will not fund your travel costs or additional fees. Some countries may require that you stay several days or weeks before returning to the United States with the adopted baby.

International adoption fees can range from $7,000 to $25,000, depending on the country's fees, your agency's fees, and your travel and stay requirements.[5] An advantage of international adoption is that you typically will know in advance how long it will take for a child to be available to you. If you're number 186 in the queue, you'll get the 186th child available. Very likely, the child will be at least four to six months old and in most cases will have lived in an orphanage. The willingness of the child's country to allow adoptions or to allow adoptions from the United States may also depend on the current governmental policy or the government's relationship with the United States at that time. Downsides include all of the above plus, depending on your ethnicity and the child's place of birth, the child might not look like you—but you most likely addressed this last issue when you first made the decision to adopt.

Adoptive Families

On the average, each year throughout the 1990s, around 120,000 children were adopted in the United States.[6] Over a ten-year period, that adds up to more than 1 million people! About 60 percent of Americans know someone who has been adopted, has adopted, or who has given up a child for adoption.[7] Most adoptive parents are in their thirties, but many successful adoptions are by older parents. Financial assistance is available to some adoptive parents, usually from domestic private agencies or from public agencies for special-needs children. Some adoption expenses are also tax deductible.

The typical family with an adopted child will be just as normal as any other family. Usually the child is told that she was adopted, and often the parents will provide the background for how the child was "picked." Other than some natural curiosity about their birth parents, adopted children can lead an otherwise ordinary life. Generally, children adopted at birth do as well as or better in social situations as their friends and are less likely to repeat a grade in school.

Two years after completing fertility treatments, my husband and I decided to look into adoption. We attended an all-day adoption workshop sponsored by RESOLVE. The seminar was extremely educational, covering all aspects of adoption: open, closed, domestic, international, legal matters, and adoption concerns, including how to deal with questions from family, friends, and coworkers. Ken and I chose to go with an adoption attorney as opposed to an adoption agency.

Our attorney had us fill out stacks of paperwork and obtain three referrals from family and friends. In addition, we were fingerprinted, had background checks, and underwent a home-study interview. About two weeks later, we were approved for adoption. We researched and talked with a number of people who had gone through open adoption and decided that was what we wanted. We wanted to stay in contact with the birth mother and allow our child to know his birth mother.

Over a twenty-one month search, we were presented with three different opportunities. The first birth mother had selected five couples, defined by income, career, and education. To us, she seemed to be auctioning her child to the highest bidder. This made us extremely uncomfortable and we chose not to participate.

The next adoption opportunity was a scam; the woman wasn't even pregnant. We conversed over the phone with the birth mother for over two months. During this time, we detected a lot of inconsistencies in what she was saying. Our attorney recommended that we schedule a meeting with her. When we did, she became very nervous, and decided to cancel all contact. The experience was disappointing, but we were thankful that we were alerted to the situation.

The third birth mother who chose us was eight months pregnant. We were so excited that we had the baby's room all set up and decorated. Then, only two weeks prior to the baby's birth, we learned of a possible health issue with the child. The news was devastating. We researched everything, talked to nurses, doctors, our home study agent, our attorney, our family and friends, and searched our own souls. In the end, we concluded the risks were too great at our age and decided not to adopt the baby. The decision was heartbreaking. We felt as if there had been a death in the family and mourned the loss of a child for over six months. Our search for a birth mother ended on our agreed-upon deadline, my forty-seventh birthday. Although we were saddened to give up our dreams of having a baby, I had promised my husband not to extend the deadline and I kept my promise.

Stacey and Greg also turned to adoption, but they had happier results. Stacey had undergone many cycles of fertility treatments that created tremendous swings of hope followed by despair. Faced with being a childless couple or a family created through adoption, Stacey and Greg chose the latter. In the end, they decided it didn't matter how their family came to be, so long as it did. They started discussing adoption before completing their last fertility treatment. They delayed their pursuit of adoption until they had had ample time to complete the grieving process for the children they never gave birth to during fertility treatments. Once they were ready, their hearts were completely open to becoming an adoptive family.

Stacey and Greg gave serious consideration to both domestic and international adoption. Ultimately, they chose domestic open adoption because it was more affordable and Stacey didn't like long flights, which an international adoption would require. Stacey and Greg were a little fearful of open adoption when they first began that stage of their journey. Through their support group, which included Stacey's brother, they met many couples that had opted for open adoption. These couples' positive experiences gave Stacey and Greg some level of peace. They realized that open adoption is not co-parenting—it is simply keeping lines of communication open. They also realized that they wouldn't be able to control the minimum level of communication, but they would be able to control the maximum. Stacey and Greg chose a level that they were comfortable with and felt would be in the best interest of their child.

After nearly sixteen months of mailing more than 150 "dear birth mother" letters and retaining an attorney, they met with and were selected by their birth mother. About two and a half months later, Stacey and

Greg were driving home from the hospital with a baby girl. A little over a year later, Stacey and Greg decided to search for another birth mother and received a number of responses to their "dear birth mother" letters, one of which was from their daughter's birth mother. From their perspective, the choice didn't even require any serious thought. They already knew, trusted, and loved this woman and could hardly believe they would have children who were siblings.

What Stacey and Greg enjoyed most about the adoption process was being a part of the RESOLVE Support Group and meeting many other couples undergoing the same process. They also appreciated knowing that, unlike with infertility treatments, in the end they would have a child. The couple enjoys being parents, and of parenthood they said, "Although words cannot describe the amount of work it is to be a parent, the amount of joy it brings is an order of magnitude greater than the work. Seeing the sheer joy on your child's face when you experience 'a first' with them is unbelievably magical." By the way, Stacey and Greg have just completed their third adoption—this time a baby boy.

Another couple, Silvia and Larry, got married in their late thirties and learned early on that both of them had infertility problems. After a brief attempt at resolving the problems, they decided to pursue adoption. For them, it wasn't a difficult decision because they truly wanted to become parents. They made their decision to adopt only nine months after first discussing the option.

At first, Silvia and Larry felt international adoption was best for them. Their reasoning was that adopting domestically meant that it would be an open adoption. This seemed too frightening and risky to them, and they were very uncomfortable with the process. However, after reading, researching, and talking with other parents who had undergone open adoption, they decided that open adoption was best for the child and all involved. Silvia and Larry pursued open adoption for their first child. There were no "red flags" in their adoption experience and they have kept in touch with the birth mother since their daughter's birth. She is now six years old.

When Silvia and Larry decided to adopt a second child, their first child was around two years old. This time, they chose to adopt internationally and they became parents to a beautiful little girl from China. The adoption was relatively quick and their daughter was healthy. Although they were told there was a possibility of obtaining birth information, unfortunately, it never materialized.

For Silvia and Larry, the adoption support group they attended was the single, most helpful part of their journey. They love parenthood and say, "Being a parent is the most awesome job you can have. Coming home and having your child come running up to you saying 'Hi, Mom,' or 'Hi, Dad,' or 'I love you' is such an incredibly joyful feeling. Being a parent is amazing!"

Adoptive parents typically have experienced some infertility issues or have age or health issues that make pregnancy unwise, and they want very much to have a child.

If you have sought help for infertility, you obviously want a child. If having your own is not possible, or if you're uncomfortable with a recommended infertility process, consider adoption. Most adoptive parents will agree that once you've held your new baby, the love and bonding process begins. True, the "birthing process" will have been different, but your maternal needs will be met (and without stretch marks!).

Chapter 17

Breaking Up

Y ou're stuck. You still want a baby and he doesn't. You have been tested and you know that you are fertile. Or you've discovered that you have or he has fertility issues, but he does not want to go through fertility treatments and procedures to try to have a child. Sometimes, no matter how hard some couples try to work out their differences, they remain at opposite ends of the spectrum. Sometimes people are so firmly planted in their convictions that they will not look at possibilities of change or exploration. In these circumstances, many couples choose to end the relationship and move on to fulfill their needs with someone else.

Before You Go

Before you get to this stage, or even if you are at this stage, you need to ask yourself if your relationship can be saved without an agreement on children. This is a huge decision, and it often means that one of you will have to make a compromise if you want to remain together. Remember, if you make a compromise of this magnitude just to appease your partner, and you still have strong urges to have children, you may become bitter and resentful, which will likely cause problems later in your relationship. Likewise, if your partner caves in and agrees to have children when he is really opposed to the idea, he may harbor feelings of resentment toward you and perhaps even toward your child. If you do compromise, make sure that both of you can live with the outcome.

If you value your relationship, and you find that you both are stonewalling, you should explore whether having children is more important to you than your marriage or relationship. This question will require some soul-searching about why you want to have a child and why it is so important to you. People mature, and often their desires and needs change. In this respect, your relationship must evolve along with these changes. (You may want to reread Chapter 2.)

Make sure that you want to have a child for the right reasons. Also, look at your relationship and determine why your partner is so important to you. There's a lot at stake here, so be sure that you're making the right choices for the right reasons.

Dr. Kovacs recommends highly that you go to a marriage and family therapist to try to work out your differences. Professional psychotherapists are better equipped to guide you through this decision-making process. Having a third-party facilitator will help keep you on track and provide an objective perspective of this complex and difficult issue. If you are married, you'll also find that counseling is a lot less expensive than getting a divorce.

Sometimes the desire to have a baby can be so consuming that some women will allow their emotional needs to overrule their marriage. Kevin and Sandy had been married ten years and were best friends and companions. The relationship appeared perfect. Their lives were filled with travel, spontaneity, evenings out, entertaining in their home, and . . . no children.

Sandy wanted children and was getting pressure from her family, so during the eighth year of their marriage, she started pushing for them to have a baby. Kevin held his ground; he had had poor childhood experiences. Sandy eventually divorced him and he was heartbroken. Sandy met and married a man that her family approved of, and now she has two beautiful children with him. She stayed in touch with Kevin and eventually confided to him that although she was very happy and loved her husband, she didn't have the closeness, the ease of discussion, or the friendship that she'd shared with Kevin. Kevin's feelings for Sandy were the same. His ex-wife has the children she always wanted, but not the husband.

The decisions we make in our lives have consequences. In Kevin's situation, his decision not to have children cost him his marriage. For Sandy, her desire to have and raise a family overruled her heart to stay in a strong, loving relationship that she now misses.

The message here is to try to work things out with your current partner until you feel you have exhausted all resources.

Re-examine your marriage or relationship and evaluate if it is the right choice for you. Ask yourself if your relationship can be saved without having agreement on children. Evaluate why having children is so important to you. Remember why you fell in love with him in the first place. How has this reason been surpassed by your need to be a mother? Determine if you are fertile before venturing off to find another partner, and ask yourself if there is time to find another while you are still fertile. Many relationships have been repaired and strengthened with the assistance of marriage and family therapists. Why not give it a try? If you find that your differences cannot be repaired, review your options and make the decision that is best for you.

Moving On

If you and your partner do sever your relationship due to irreconcilable differences on having children, you need to look at your separation as a learning experience. Perhaps you will have a better idea of what is important to you and what to look for in a future partner:

+ His thoughts on having children
+ His ability to communicate with you
+ His ability to resolve issues with you

Talking about your childhoods may give you a good idea of whether he is open to children. As your relationship progresses, you'll be able to determine if you can both resolve smaller issues. Take things slowly and try to overcome the mistakes you made in your last relationship.

Although some women are lucky at love, many discover that finding another partner can take two or three years or even longer. For older women whose biological clocks are on constant alarm, two or three years can seem an eternity. Women who are obsessed about their reproductive window of opportunity may appear anxious about the relationship's progress, and this anxiety can scare off a prospective mate. Even though these women may not say so, they may be giving strong signals: "Get me pregnant! Get me pregnant! Get me pregnant!" If this is the case, your potential partner could be running in the opposite direction faster than lightning hits an iron rod during a storm.

Even if you are lucky enough to find another partner, second marriages have about a 60 percent divorce rate.[1] Dr. Kovacs has found that if a partner hasn't resolved issues from the first marriage, there is a high probability that those same issues will arise in the second marriage.

Some women who have broken off a relationship due to the child issue decide to go it alone and have a child without a partner. According to the Centers for Disease Control and Prevention and the National Center for Health Statistics, in the year 2001, 33.5 percent of births were to unmarried women aged fifteen and over. Out of those, 17.1 percent of births were to unmarried women who were forty years and older.[2]

Interestingly, the U.S. Department of Health and Human Services reported that 33 percent of adopted children are adopted by a single parent; the majority of the adoptive parents are female.[3] We speculate that many of these women chose to have a child alone rather than stay in a relationship with a partner who was not open to children. Their desire to have a family and their need to nurture another was stronger than their desire to remain in an unsupportive relationship. However, unmarried women can and do have children, either through pregnancy or adoption. This trend is climbing and should be considered a viable option, provided you want a child, have the means to support the child, and have the patience, love, and understanding it takes to raise a child.

If you decide that moving on is the best option, remember to think positively and appreciate what you have learned from the process.

Chapter 18

Closure

We hope that with this book and other tools, you and your partner have overcome your differences about whether to have children, you've reached an amicable agreement on the issue, and you've enriched your relationship throughout the process. If you are still in the throes of the decision-making process, review Parts I and II as if you are following a recipe.

Use the communication tools and sample questions to address practical considerations about children. Take a step back from where you are today and re-examine what it means to have a child. Wanting a child and being able to raise a child successfully are two different issues. Look deep within yourself to know why you want a child, what needs you believe having this child would fulfill for you, and what you could offer the child. With this analysis also comes the other side of the equation . . . your partner. Once you have a clear understanding of how you feel about being a mother, explore what his feelings are toward fatherhood. The two of you also want to look at what you could offer your baby, and you need to begin to work out a process to get to a successful agreement.

Successful resolution of this issue will depend on how you approach the subject and when. Feelings about children may be identified early in your relationship by discussing your families, your memories of growing up, your brothers and sisters, and your nieces and nephews. If your partner has had a healthy family experience, it is a good (but not absolute) indication that he could be open to having children. Remember that being open and honest, from the very beginning of your relationship, will give you a strong foundation to build upon.

Sharing your values and beliefs will also allow you to see if there is compatibility or conflict in other areas. This is a huge decision that will affect you both for the rest of your lives, so take things slowly and don't rush through your decision.

Depending on your circumstances, you and your partner may want to refer back to the various couples' examples in this book. Look for possible solutions you can use in your situation. By stepping back and examining other couples' conflicts, you will get a better sense of what you can do to help your own.

You may eventually decide that you no longer want children. Whether you decide that your relationship is more important than your need to have a child, or you face health issues that make childbearing risky, you will need to address the emotional loss of not being able to have a biological child. Remember, the younger you are when you choose a permanent form of birth control, such as a tubal ligation, the more likely you are to regret it later on. The one thing that is certain in life is change and circumstances may bring unexpected changes into your life. Maybe your partner will change his mind in a few years, or maybe there will be a new "he" later on in your life and you will change your mind. If you do decide to remain childless, you will need to address your maternal emotional needs, but you can still have a very fulfilling life without children.

Whether you have reached an impasse in your conflict, discovered a problem that you cannot handle alone, or want some guidance to help you progress more productively, seeing a trained professional is a good idea.

As in any relationship-challenging situation, there are different outcomes for your situation. Many couples that have successfully resolved their differences on the decision to have children find that they have improved their communications skills and have a more satisfying relationship because of the ordeal. No matter what your decision, if you can successfully resolve this conflict, you will significantly increase the success and closeness of your relationship. In addition, the communication skills you learned along the way may help you in other avenues of your life . . . dealing with work conflicts, nasty neighbors, and your mother-in-law, to name a few.

We hope you will get your wish. Recognize that when you have a child, your relationship will change. He'll get less attention, both of you will be more tired, and things will be . . . well, different! Baby makes three, but don't forget that one and two are also important.

If circumstances leave you child-free, there are a number of things that you can do to accept your situation—I know this from personal experience. Find other avenues to fill your need to nurture.

If nature isn't cooperating once you've convinced him to have a child, you can choose to adopt. Although the process can seem mind-boggling at times, professionals can help you through. There are many children out there who need a nice home.

Finally, you may find that your need to become a mother is greater than your desire to remain in your relationship. Not all couples are able to reach an amicable agreement on their differences about children, no matter how hard they try. If this happens, breaking up and moving forward with your life may be much more satisfying than staying in a relationship in which your needs cannot be met. Be thankful that there are no children involved, be confident that you are doing what is best for you, and make sure that you don't forget all the things that you have learned. Going forward, you will have a better idea of what to look for when you begin dating and how to communicate when discussing sensitive items, and you will know from experience what doesn't work.

No matter what your outcome, acknowledge that you have succeeded because you have chosen to resolve your relationship's conflict on this issue. You are now more aware of your needs, know how to communicate them to your partner, and have the ability to resolve one of the most difficult conflicts two people can face.

Appendix

Suggested Reading

A Baby? . . . Maybe (1980), by Dr. Elizabeth M. Whelan, Sc.D.

Adopting after Infertility (1994), by Patricia Irwin Johnston

Adopting in California (1999), by Randall Hicks

Adoption Without Fear (1989), by James L. Gritter, M.S.W.

Childlessness Transformed: Stories of Alternative Parenting (1989), by Jane English

Children of Open Adoption (1990), by Kathleen Silber and Patricia Martinez Dorner

Conjoint Family Therapy (1983), by Virginia Satir

The Couple's Guide to Fertility (2001), by Gary S. Berger, M.D., Marc Goldstein, M.D., and Mark Fuerst

Fighting for Your Marriage (2001), by Howard J. Markman, Scott M. Stanley, and Susan L. Blumberg

Fishing By Moonlight, The Art of Choosing Intimate Partners (1996), by Colene Sawyer, Ph.D.

Going It Alone: Meeting the Challenges of Being a Single Mom (1999), by Michele Howe

The Parent Test (1978), by Ellen Peck and Dr. William Granzig

The Parenthood Decision (1998), by Beverly Engel

Parenting an Only Child: The Joys and Challenges of Raising Your One and Only (1990), by Susan Newman

The Seven Principles for Making Marriage Work (2000), by John M. Gottman, Ph.D., and Nan Silver

The Single Child Family (1984), by Dr. Toni Falbo

Single Mothers by Choice: A Guidebook for Single Women Who Are Considering or Have Chosen Motherhood (1997), by Jane Mattes

The Transition to Parenthood: How a First Child Changes a Marriage— Why Some Couples Grow Closer and Others Apart (1995), by Jay Belsky, Ph.D., and John Kelly

Unwomanly Conduct: The Challenges of Intentional Childlessness (1994), by Carolyn M. Morell

What to Expect When You're Experiencing Infertility: How to Cope with the Emotional Crisis and Survive (1998), by Debbie Peoples and Harriette Rovner Ferguson

Why Don't You Have Kids? (1995), by Leslie Lafayette

Without Child: Challenging the Stigma of Childlessness (1999), by Laurie Lisle

Recommended Organizations for Assistance

American Association for Marriage and Family Therapy
AAMFT
112 South Alfred St.
Alexandria, VA 22314-3061
Phone: 703-838-9808
www.aamft.org

The American Association for Marriage and Family Therapy contains helpful information as well as listings for member therapists in your area. At the time of this writing, you had to click on each therapist's link to determine his or her specialty.

Planned Parenthood Federation of America
434 West 33rd St.
New York, NY 10001
Phone: 1-800-230-PLAN
www.plannedparenthood.org

Planned Parenthood centers are located throughout the United States and provide counseling services and information to help you. Check your local telephone book for nearby contact numbers.

RESOLVE, the National Infertility Association
1310 Broadway
Somerville, MA 02144
Toll-Free Help: 888-623-0744
www.resolve.org
RESOLVE has chapters throughout the United States and has excellent information on infertility issues. Their local chapters also sponsor informative seminars on infertility and adoption.

Society for Assisted Reproductive Technology (SART)
1209 Montgomery Highway
Birmingham, AL 35216
Phone: 205-978-5000
www.sart.org
SART's Web site includes a "Find a Clinic" section that lists most of the fertility clinics in the United States. SART also is a major feeder of statistics to the Center for Disease Control and Prevention's reporting.

Stepfamily Foundation, Inc.
333 West End Avenue
New York, NY 10023
Phone: 212-877-3244
Fax: 212-362-7030
www.stepfamily.org
The Stepfamily Foundation offers professional counseling, via phone, to help create and maintain a successful stepfamily bond. They also provide stepfamily support materials, and their Web site offers a Couple Questionnaire.

Web Sites for Additional Information

http://adopting.adoption.com/child/self-assessment-adoption-quiz.html
Offers a self-assessment adoption quiz.

www.ivillage.com Offers information on all types of women's issues, pregnancy, fertility, children, parenting, health, relationships, and more.

www.nokidding.net For people who are childless. No Kidding has chapters throughout the United States and Canada (and the world!).

www.parentsplace.com Offers family therapist articles by Gayle Peterson, M.S.S.W., Ph.D.

www.psychologytoday.com For use in finding a therapist (click on "Find a Therapist" located under the Toolbox section); provides access to lots of information on therapy, relationships, etc.

www.teenageparent.org/english/costofbaby2B.html Helps calculate first-year baby expenses based on your selection of items.

Parenting
Questionnaire

How to Be a Good Parent

In order to be good parents, we must have realistic expectations. Do we? Here's a quick reality check on what being a good parent is about.

Reality Check—What to Expect

Realistic	Unrealistic	
❏	❏	Being a good parent will come naturally.
❏	❏	Having a child will make everything in my life fall into place.
❏	❏	I won't have problems with my child if I love my child enough.
❏	❏	My child will give me all the love I need.
❏	❏	My child will be happy if I'm a good parent.
❏	❏	Everything will go smoothly if I try hard enough.
❏	❏	My kids will grow up to be what I want them to be.

You get an "A" if you understand that all of these expectations are unrealistic. Women and men with unrealistic expectations may not be prepared for the real work of parenthood.

Being a good parent takes work. The job is to help children to grow up to fulfill their potential in life. It takes lots of patience and understanding, but it offers great rewards—for our kids, for ourselves, and for our communities. The better we understand the job, the better we can do it.

It is a delicate balancing act to take care of our own needs and our children's as well. We can be proud of ourselves whenever we manage to do it.

Taking Care of Children's Basic Needs

We all have basic needs that must be met before we can realize our dreams. Until our kids can meet their own needs, we must do it for them. We must also help them learn how to take care of themselves.

There are six levels of basic needs.* Each level supports the next—like the layers of a pyramid. If the needs at one level are not met, it may be very difficult to move up to the next.

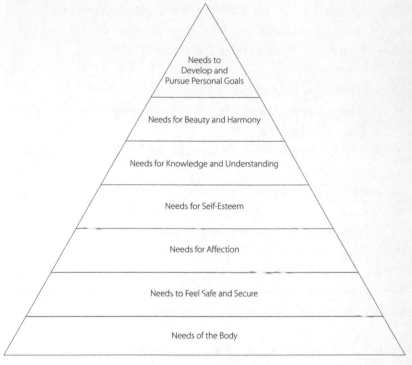

Needs to Develop and Pursue Personal Goals

Needs for Beauty and Harmony

Needs for Knowledge and Understanding

Needs for Self-Esteem

Needs for Affection

Needs to Feel Safe and Secure

Needs of the Body

These basic concepts are based on Dr. Abraham Maslow's hierarchy of needs theory.

All these needs continue throughout life. It can take a lifetime of effort for children and parents to reach the top of the pyramid. Some never do. It takes great patience, good communication, lots of love, and good luck. There are no guarantees. Even very good parents need to be prepared for disappointments.

We all make mistakes. But the more we understand the job, and the harder we try to do it well, the more likely it is that our kids will reach their greatest potential.

Level One—Meeting Our Children's Bodily Needs

We couldn't live without nutritious food, clean water and air, and regular sleep. We must also feel good about and take pleasure in our bodies and sexuality. We give babies a sense of themselves, their sexuality, and their bodies from birth. We make them feel secure or insecure by

+ The way we hold and touch them
+ The way we feed, wash, diaper, and toilet train them
+ The tone of voice we use
+ Letting them feel comfortable with their bodies and emotions

Kids have healthier feelings if we do these things in a pleasant and caring way.

It's normal for babies to explore their bodies. They are quick to learn that touching themselves—especially their sex organs—feels good. If we yell at them or slap their hands, they may do it anyway—but they'll feel guilty about it. They may become ashamed of their bodies and sexuality. And they may not trust us later in life for guidance about sex and sexuality.

Level One Reality Check—Needs of the Body

Realistic   Unrealistic

❏   ❏   I can provide my child with nutritious food.

❏   ❏   My routine will allow my child to get plenty of sleep regularly.

❏   ❏   I can keep my child clean.

❏   ❏   I can be sure my child receives regular medical care.

❏   ❏   I can comfort my child when she or he needs to relieve stress and anxiety by crying.

❏   ❏   I can acknowledge that my child is a sexual being.

These are all realistic goals for good parents. Parents who try to meet these basic "level one" needs help their children go on to develop needs for feeling safe and secure.

Level Two—
Meeting Our Children's Needs to Feel Safe and Secure

We all need protection from physical harm and freedom from fear.

We are often the people our children fear most. Our kids depend on us, and they often worry about whether we will be there for them.

How we deal with anger has a lot to do with how safe and secure our children feel. We must set good examples of love and compassion. When troubles arise or mistakes are made we must be able to

+ be patient and reasonable
+ keep the "lines" of communication open to say, "I am so angry I'm afraid I'll hurt your feelings. Give me a few minutes to calm down, and then we can talk."

Our good examples help our kids express anger and frustration in healthy ways.

Level Two Reality Check—Needs for Safety and Security

Realistic	*Unrealistic*	
❑	❑	I can provide a safe comfortable place to live.
❑	❑	I can provide a good model of self-control when I'm angry by taking time out to calm down.
❑	❑	I won't use physical force or threats.
❑	❑	I can talk about my point of view without accusing my child.
❑	❑	I can take responsibility for my own emotions and can offer support and consolation to my child, no matter how angry I am or how frightened my child may be.

These are all realistic goals for good parents. Parents who try to meet these basic "level two" needs help their children go on to develop needs for affection.

Level Three—
Meeting Our Children's Needs for Affection

All children want, need, and deserve unconditional love. Children thrive on affection—emotional attachment, fondness, love, and devotion. Kids have a great need to love and be loved. They also need to know that they belong—and will always have a place in their families and communities, no matter what.

Children learn about affection from the examples we set. We show them how people who care about each other get along with one another. They imitate what we do and what we are, not what we want to be.

Affection between family members increases their joy and pleasure in life. Kids from affectionate families are better equipped to cope with the frustrations and disappointments of daily life. They also can more easily work and play to pursue common goals.

Level Three Reality Check—Needs for Affection

Realistic *Unrealistic*

❑ ❑ I can give my child unconditional love and physical affection.

❑ ❑ I can provide a model for loving, respectful, and caring behavior.

❑ ❑ I can help my child talk about, understand, and trust her or his feelings and needs.

❑ ❑ I can accept my child as an individual whose feelings and needs are different from mine.

❑ ❑ I can reward caring and affectionate behavior with caring and affectionate attention.

These are all realistic goals for good parents. Parents who try to meet these basic "level three" needs help their children go on to develop needs for self-esteem.

Level Four—
Meeting Our Children's Needs for Self-Esteem

Self-esteem begins with receiving unconditional love and support—especially from parents. Kids really want to know that they're "normal." We must teach them that it is "normal" to be different. Giving our kids a sense of worth, competence, and normality will also help them develop respect for others.

Praise is the best way to teach self-esteem. We should praise honesty, independence, talent, effort, fair play, and kindness. We erode our kids' self-esteem when we ridicule, humiliate, or hit them.

Offering options instead of giving orders lets them become good decision makers, too. Begin with small choices, for example, ask if they want pasta or burgers for supper. Let the decisions get bigger as the child gets older.

Level Four Reality Check—Needs for Self-Esteem

Realistic	Unrealistic	
❏	❏	I am more likely to praise than criticize my child.
❏	❏	I reward positive behavior.
❏	❏	I believe mistakes are good opportunities to provide positive learning experiences.
❏	❏	I can help my child learn to be proud of her or his body, appearance, talents, and intellect.
❏	❏	I can help my child take pride in her or his moral values, behaviors, and relationships.
❏	❏	I can apologize to my child.
❏	❏	I can offer my child reasonable alternatives, instead of commands.

These are all realistic goals for good parents. Parents who try to meet these basic "level four" needs help their children go on to develop needs for knowledge and understanding.

Level Five—
Meeting Our Children's Needs for Knowledge and Understanding

Good parents provide experiences and opportunities that stimulate a child's thirst for knowledge and understanding, which are essential for successful lives.

We must reward children with approval when they learn something new. We must provide daily opportunities for learning. School, hobbies, family projects, working and playing together, household chores, shopping, camp, clubs, movies, plays, concerts, sports, nature hikes, museums, trips, and outings are all valuable learning experiences for children.

Level Five Reality Check—Needs for Knowledge and Understanding

Realistic   Unrealistic

❏   ❏   I can reward my child for asking questions and support interests that are different from mine.

❏   ❏   I can provide information and support during the changes of growing up.

❏   ❏   I can patiently help my child with homework.

❏   ❏   I can teach and play games with my child.

❏   ❏   I can let my child win.

❏   ❏   I can include my child in conversations with adults.

❏   ❏   I can provide my child with varied social outlets.

❏   ❏   I can be available whenever she or he wants to talk.

These are all realistic goals for good parents. Parents who try to meet these basic "level five" needs help their children go on to develop needs for knowledge and understanding.

Level Six—
Meeting Our Children's Needs for Beauty and Harmony

We all have a need for beauty and harmony in our lives. This includes music and art, the natural world, our moral and spiritual beliefs, our social customs, our cultural heritage, and an appreciation for positive, caring, intimate relationships with other people. They all provide us with a sense of balance and allow us to have hope for the future.

Level Six Reality Check—Needs for Beauty and Harmony

Realistic   Unrealistic

❏	❏	I can share my dreams with my child and encourage my child to dream.
❏	❏	I can help my child appreciate the beauty of nature.
❏	❏	I can create an orderly family environment that includes arts and crafts.
❏	❏	I can encourage my child to be creative—draw, paint, write, play an instrument, sing, or dance.
❏	❏	I can accept that my child will develop tastes and a personal style different from my own.
❏	❏	I can help my child appreciate the value of keeping physically fit.

These are all realistic goals for good parents. Parents who try to meet these basic "level six" needs help their children go on to acquire the need to develop and pursue personal goals.

Level Seven—
The Need to Develop and Pursue Personal Goals

When our children attain the need to develop and pursue their own meaningful goals, they are on their way to independence. We all reach this stage at different times in our lives—if we reach it at all. Some people never do. Unfortunately, it's often a daily effort just to satisfy more basic levels of need. If basic levels of need are never met, it is very difficult to progress to higher needs.

Parents who have helped their children reach the seventh level—independence—have good reason to be proud.

Self-Discipline and Punishment

Our children need to know how to balance their individual needs with the needs of others. This takes self-discipline. Self-discipline is knowing how to behave within the rules. It's our job to coach our children to understand moral values and follow rules inside and outside the home.

Reasoning is always better than punishment as a way to keep children from breaking rules. Asking a child to take "time out" to think about her or his behavior is often helpful. Here are some guidelines for the rare occasions when punishment may be unavoidable. Effective punishment

+ Is about the child's behavior, not about the child's character. The message is, "What you did was wrong," not, "You're a rotten kid!"
+ Is limited to a situation in which a rule was broken
+ Immediately follows the breaking of the rule
+ Is done calmly
+ Does not include the withdrawal of love and affection
+ Is not an assertion of a parent's power, anger, or frustration
+ Includes explanations that do not give mixed messages
+ Includes a penalty—a "time out" or temporary loss of privilege
+ Does not inflict physical or emotional pain
+ Is brief

Joys and Rewards

If you decide to become a parent, you will probably have to learn to cope with pain, conflict, and sorrow. They are often part of the parenthood experience. But you will also probably experience many joys and rewards. They are all possible regardless of our own experience with our own parents.

Here are some of the joys and rewards women and men say they receive by being parents—they

+ Gain satisfaction with life
+ Learn about themselves through their children
+ Receive love and affection
+ Find a creative outlet
+ Feel they become "really" adult
+ Discover a sense of achievement
+ Fulfill their family values
+ Fulfill their need for a family
+ Resolve issues of their own childhood
+ Put their own lives into perspective
+ Become better communicators
+ More deeply appreciate the past and future
+ Have deeper understanding of other people
+ Delight in physical contact with their children
+ Delight in playing with their children
+ Delight in witnessing their children develop skills
+ Value companionship with their children
+ Value the emotional closeness that can develop
+ Delight in the happiness and laughter of children
+ Delight in watching children develop independence and mature concern for others

When to Have a Child

Deciding to become a parent is one thing. Deciding when to become a parent is another.

Whether you are planning a pregnancy or having an unplanned pregnancy, whether you have a partner or plan to have a partner or plan to be a single parent, here are some considerations about deciding if it's time to have a child. If there are two of you, see if your reality checks match.

Reality Check—When to Have a Child

Realistic	Unrealistic	
❑	❑	I am ready to help a child feel wanted and loved.
❑	❑	I am ready to cope with tighter budgets, less time for myself, and more stress.
❑	❑	I communicate well with my partner, family, and friends.
❑	❑	I will be able to keep from harming the child physically or emotionally.
❑	❑	I am ready to come to terms with my own childhood experience.
❑	❑	I have the support of family and friends.
❑	❑	I am not rigid about how to solve problems.
❑	❑	I am ready to accept responsibility to try and meet all the levels of need my child develops.

Endnotes

PART I—APPROACHING THE SUBJECT

Chapter 1: How to Begin Talking about Children

1. Virginia Satir, *Conjoint Family Therapy* (Palo Alto, CA: Science and Behavior Books, 1983)
2. "Falling in Love . . . The Magic," DiscoveryHealth.com, 2004 *http://health.discovery.com*

Chapter 2: Practical Considerations about Children

1. IRS information as of 2004 at *www.irs.gov.*
2. USDA, "Expenditures on Children by Families," 2003, Center for Nutrition Policy and Promotion, Miscellaneous Publication Number 1528-2003.
3. "Preconception, Practical Considerations," *www.ninemonths. com*, et al.

Chapter 3: Setting the Ground Rules

1. John M. Gottman, Ph.D., and Nan Silver, *The Seven Principles for Making Marriage Work* (New York, NY: Three Rivers Press, 2000), pp. 130–132.

PART II—DEALING WITH THE CONFLICT

Chapter 4: Overcoming Fears

1. National Fatherhood Initiative, Wade F. Horn, Ph.D., and Tom Sylvester, *www.fatherhood.org*, *Father Facts: 4th Edition*, 2002.

Chapter 5: When He's Not Saying "No" but "Not Yet"

1. John M. Gottman, Ph.D., and Nan Silver, *The Seven Principles for Making Marriage Work* (New York, NY: Three Rivers Press, 2000), pp. 130–132.
2. Ibid, pp. 26–27.

Chapter 6: Additional Children

1. U.S. Census Bureau report, "Women Aged 40–44 by Number of Children They've Ever Born," Internet release date October 23, 2003.
2. Bao-Ping Zhu, M.D., Robert T. Rolfs, M.D., M.P.H., Barry E. Nangle, Ph.D., and John M. Horan, M.D., M.P.H., "Effect of the Interval between Pregnancies on Perinatal Outcomes," *The New England Journal of Medicine* (Feb. 25, 1999) vol. 340, pp. 589–594.
3. Dr. Gayle Peterson, M.F.T., in her column for ParentsPlace. com. Additional data from a study by the University of California at San Francisco, published May 7, 1998.
4. Studies by Dr. Toni Falbo of the University of Texas-Austin and author of *The Single Child Family* (New York, NY: Guilford Press, 1984).

Chapter 7: Second Marriages

1. Data on divorce and remarriage from the 2002 U.S. Census Bureau's report titled, "Number, Timing, and Duration of Marriages and Divorces, 1996."
2. U.S. Divorce Statistics, *www.DivorceMagazine.com*.

Chapter 8: The V Word—Vasectomies

1. Dr. Werthman, Center for Male Reproductive Medicine, "Vasectomy Reversal," *www.malereproduction.com*.
2. Ibid.
3. Center for Male Reproductive Medicine, *http://www.malerepro duction.com/08_vasectomyrev.html*.

Chapter 9: Agreeing Not to Have Children

1. U.S. Census Bureau report, "Women Aged 40–44 by Number of Children They've Ever Born," Internet release date October 23, 2003.
2. "National Center for Health Statistics New Report Documents Trends in Childbearing," *Reproductive Health*, June 5, 1997.
3. Larry L. Bumpass, Ph.D., Elizabeth Thomson, Ph.D., and Amy L. Godecker, M.S., Center for Demography and Ecology, University of Wisconsin-Madison, "Women, Men, and Contraceptive Sterilization," *Fertility and Sterility* vol. 73, no. 5, May 2000.
4. National Center for Chronic Disease Prevention and Health Promotion, CDS's Reproductive Health Information Source, Unintended Pregnancy, "Surgical Sterilization in the United States: Prevalence and Characteristics," 1965–1995, *Vital and Health Statistics Series* 23/no.20.

5. Ibid.
6. Bradley Van Voorhis, M.D., "Tubal Ligation Reversal," Virtual Hospital: a digital library of health information, *www.vh.org.* "Tubal Ligation Reversal," UAB Health System, *www.health.uab. edu.*
7. Vasovasostomy costs gathered from Web sites of various clinics.
8. Philip Wise, "Male Infertility Update," *Western Journal of Medicine*, December 1991, p. 635.
9. IVF costs gathered from Web sites of various clinics.
10. "Adoption Disruption and Dissolution: Numbers and Trends," The National Adoption Information Clearinghouse, U.S. Department of Health & Human Services—Administration for Children & Families, *http://naic.acf.hhs.gov.*

Chapter 10: Becoming Pregnant Against His Wishes

1. Planned Parenthood® Federation of America, Inc., "Birth Control, Your Contraceptive Choices," PPFA Web site © 1998–2004 Planned Parenthood® Federation of America, Inc.
2. Ibid.
3. Tracy Quan, "Conception by Deception," article for Salon.com, September 23, 1998.

PART III—OUTCOMES

Chapter 12: The Key to a Satisfying Relationship: Communication

1. Virginia P. Richmond, James C. McCroskey, and K. David Roach, "Communication and Decision-Making Styles, Power Base Usage, and Satisfaction in Marital Dyads," *www.jamescmc roskey.com/publications/171.htm*.
2. John M. Gottman, Ph.D., and Nan Silver, *The Seven Principles for Making Marriage Work* (New York, NY: Three Rivers Press, 2000), pp. 26–27.
3. Jay Belsky, Ph.D, and John Kelly, *The Transition to Parenthood: How a First Child Changes a Marriage—Why Some Couples Grow Closer and Others Apart* (New York, NY: Bantam Doubleday Dell Publishing Group, Inc., 1995), pp 6–7. Used by permission of Dell Publishing, a division of Random House, Inc.

Chapter 13: Deciding to Have Children

1. Jay Belsky, Ph.D., and John Kelly, *The Transition to Parenthood: How a First Child Changes a Marriage—Why Some Couples Grow Closer and Others Apart* (New York, NY: Bantam Doubleday Dell Publishing Group, Inc., 1995), pp. 12–16, pp. 178.

Chapter 14: Living Child-Free

1. U.S. Census Bureau, "Current Population Survey," June 2002.
2. SD Hillis et al., "Poststerilization Regret: Findings From the United States Collaborative Review of Sterilization," *Obstetrics and Gynecology*, 1999, 93(6), pp. 889–895.

Chapter 15: Treating Infertility

1. David Barad, M.D., "Age and Female Infertility," The American Infertility Association, ivillagehealth.com article.
2. Mark Perole, "Age & Fertility," ivillagehealth.com article.
3. Joan Liebmann-Smith, Ph.D., Jacqueline Nardi Egan, and John Stangel, M.D., *The Unofficial Guide to Overcoming Infertility* (New York, NY: Macmillan General Reference, 1999), p. 33–34. Robert L. Barbieri, M.D., Alice D. Domar, Ph.D., and Kevin R. Loughlin, M.D., *6 Steps to Increased Fertility* (New York, NY: Simon & Schuster, 2000), p. 46.
4. National Center on Birth Defects and Developmental Disabilities, "Birth Defects: Frequently Asked Questions (FAQs)," *www.cdc.gov/ncbddd/bd/faq1.htm.*
5. Patricia Hittner, "Starting a Family at 40," *Better Homes and Gardens,* August 1995, p. 61. Nancy L. Snyderman, M.D., and Margaret Blackstone, *Dr. Nancy Snyderman's Guide to Good Health for Women over Forty* (New York: William Morrow & Company, 1996), pp. 130, 137.
6. Joan Liebmann-Smith, Ph.D., Jacqueline Nardi Egan, and John Stangel, M.D., *The Unofficial Guide to Overcoming Infertility* (New York, NY: Macmillan General Reference, 1999), p. 345. "The Infertility Q & A: Basic Testing with a Reproductive Endochronologist," prepared by the InterNational Council on Infertility Dissemination, *www.inciid.org.*
7. Robert L. Barbieri, M.D., Alice D. Domar, Ph.D., and Kevin R. Loughlin, M.D., *6 Steps to Increased Fertility* (New York, NY: Simon & Schuster, 2000), pp. 27–28. Nancy L. Snyderman, M.D., and Margaret Blackstone, *Dr. Nancy Snyderman's Guide to Good Health for Women over Forty* (New York: William Morrow & Company, 1996), p. 130.
8. Infertility Myths and Facts, RESOLVE, *www.resolve.org.*

9. Helane S. Rosenberg, Ph.D., and Yakov M. Epstein, Ph.D., *Getting Pregnant When You Thought You Couldn't* (Warner Books, 1993, 2001), pp. 103–105; and Robert L. Barbieri, M.D., Alice D. Domar, Ph.D., and Kevin R. Loughlin, M.D., *6 Steps to Increased Fertility* (New York, NY: Simon & Schuster, 2000), pp. 135–136.

10. Joan Liebmann-Smith, Ph.D., Jacqueline Nardi Egan, and John Stangel, M.D., *The Unofficial Guide to Overcoming Infertility* (New York, NY: Macmillan General Reference, 1999), p. 91–92; 113–114.

11. Joan Liebmann-Smith, Ph.D., Jacqueline Nardi Egan, and John Stangel, M.D., *The Unofficial Guide to Overcoming Infertility* (New York, NY: Macmillan General Reference, 1999), pp. 86–87; 91–92. Helane S. Rosenberg, Ph.D., and Yakov M. Epstein, Ph.D., *Getting Pregnant When You Thought You Couldn't* (Warner Books, 1993, 2001), pp. 182–183; p. 348.

12. Gail Hendrickson, RN, BS, "Male Infertility," Diseases and Conditions Encyclopedia, *http://health.discovery.com*.

13. Joan Liebmann-Smith, Ph.D., Jacqueline Nardi Egan, and John Stangel, M.D., *The Unofficial Guide to Overcoming Infertility* (New York, NY: Macmillan General Reference, 1999), pp. 112–115. Robert L. Barbieri, M.D., Alice D. Domar, Ph.D., and Kevin R. Loughlin, M.D., *6 Steps to Increased Fertility* (New York, NY: Simon & Schuster, 2000), p. 141.

14. Joan Liebmann-Smith, Ph.D., Jacqueline Nardi Egan, and John Stangel, M.D., *The Unofficial Guide to Overcoming Infertility* (New York, NY: Macmillan General Reference, 1999), pp. 115–117.

15. Helane S. Rosenberg, Ph.D., and Yakov M. Epstein, Ph.D., *Getting Pregnant When You Thought You Couldn't* (Warner Books, 1993, 2001), pp. 126–127. "Strong Fertility and Reproductive Science Center," Pergonal (Menotropins), Strong Health, *www.stronghealth.com*.

16. Helane S. Rosenberg, Ph.D., and Yakov M. Epstein, Ph.D., *Getting Pregnant When You Thought You Couldn't* (Warner Books, 1993, 2001), pp. 141–145. Joan Liebmann-Smith, Ph.D., Jacqueline Nardi Egan, and John Stangel, M.D., *The Unofficial Guide to Overcoming Infertility* (New York, NY: Macmillan General Reference, 1999), pp. 119–122. Elaine Herscher, senior editor at *Consumer Health Interactive*, "Insemination, Pregnancy, Consumer Health Interactive," *http://blueprint.bluecrossmn.com.*

17. Joan Liebmann-Smith, Ph.D., Jacqueline Nardi Egan, and John Stangel, M.D., *The Unofficial Guide to Overcoming Infertility* (New York, NY: Macmillan General Reference, 1999), pp. 152–154. Robert L. Barbieri, M.D., Alice D. Domar, Ph.D., and Kevin R. Loughlin, M.D., *6 Steps to Increased Fertility* (New York, NY: Simon & Schuster, 2000), pp. 207–221.

18. U.S. Dept. of Health and Human Services, 2001, "Assisted Reproductive Technology Success Rates."

19. IVF Costs gathered from Web sites of various clinics.

20. Philip Wise, "Male Infertility Update," *Western Journal of Medicine*, December 1991, p. 635.

21. Vasovasostomy costs gathered from Web sites of various clinics.

22. Sherman J. Silber, M.D., "Sperm Aspiration for ICSI," The Infertility Center of Saint Louis, *www.infertile.com.*

23. Bradley Van Voorhis, M.D., "Tubal Ligation Reversal," Virtual Hospital: a digital library of health information, *www.vh.org.* "Tubal Ligation Reversal," UAB Health System, *www.health. uab.edu.*

24. Elaine Herscher, senior editor at *Consumer Health Interactive*, "Insemination, Pregnancy, Consumer Health Interactive," *http://blueprint.bluecrossmn.com.*

25. "Top Quality Egg Donors for Patients from throughout the United States and Abroad," Genetics & IVF Institute, *www.donoregg1.com.*

26. "Donor Egg Refund Guarantee Options," Genetics & IVF Institute, *www.givf.com*.

27. Joan Liebmann-Smith, Ph.D., Jacqueline Nardi Egan, and John Stangel, M.D., *The Unofficial Guide to Overcoming Infertility* (New York, NY: Macmillan General Reference, 1999), pp. 204–205.

Chapter 16: Adoption as an Option

1. "Review of Qualification Requirements for Prospective Adoptive Parents," *http://adopting.adoption.com*.

2. "Adoption Disruption and Dissolution: Numbers and Trends," The National Adoption Information Clearinghouse, U.S. Department of Health & Human Services—Administration for Children & Families, *http://naic.acf.hhs.gov*.

3. Ibid.

4. Ibid.

5. Ibid.

6. Ibid.

7. The Evan B. Donaldson Adoption Institute, "Overview of Adoption in the United States," *www.adoptioninstitute.org*.

Chapter 17: Breaking Up

1. "U.S. Divorce Statistics," DivorceMagazine.com.

2. "Births to Unmarried Women: Percentage of All Births That Are to Unmarried Women by Age of Mother, Selected Years 1980–2001," Centers for Disease Control and Prevention, National Center for Health Statistics, National Vital Statistics System.

3. "Single Adoptive Parents," The National Adoption Information Clearinghouse, U.S. Department of Health & Human Services, *http://naic.acf.hhs.gov*.

Index

About the Authors

DONNA J. WADE has successfully faced the challenge addressed in *I Want a Baby, He Doesn't* with her husband. She first told her family's story in a self-published book. Through extensive world travel, Donna has performed volunteer work as an editor in a newsletter for the American Women's Club in Lausanne, Switzerland. She lives in Sacramento, California, with her husband, Ken, and their Dalmatian, Bella.

LIBERTY KOVACS, Ph.D., M.F.T., is a licensed marital/family therapist and holds a Ph.D. in marital/family therapy from the California Graduate School of Family Psychology. Dr. Kovacs has published articles about marriage in a number of professional journals and mainstream publications, such as *Family Therapy*, *The Sacramento Bee*, *Body and Soul*, and *Good Housekeeping*, London. Dr. Kovacs lives in Sacramento, California.